2001

# A Few Marbles Left

# A Few Marbles Left

## A Close-Up Look at TV News
## in All Its Agonizing, Maddening Lunacy
## (and Its Occasional Moments of Glory)

### John Corcoran

#### Foreword by Mervin Block

*Bonus Books, Inc.*
*Chicago, Illinois*

05  04  03  02  01                                5  4  3  2  1

Library of Congress Control Number: 2001092827

ISBN: 1-56625-167-2

Bonus Books, Inc.
160 East Illinois Street
Chicago, IL  60611

Printed in the United States of America

*To my family—and all the families.*

*Television is a triumph of equipment over people, and the minds that control it are so small that you could put them in a gnat's navel with room left over for two caraway seeds and an agent's heart.*

—Fred Allen

# Table of Contents

# Foreword
## by Mervin Block

Are you a TV critic? Everyone else is. Even people who don't have a TV. *Especially* people who don't have a TV. Most people working in TV, even those on air, don't criticize TV publicly. Certainly not the folks working at networks; they don't want to foul their own nets.

But people who *used to* work in TV can be very vocal. Take John Corcoran. He used to dance on TV—until he scratched the set. Now he's jumping on TV, more or less, mostly more. In *A Few Marbles Left*, he has a lot to say about TV news, and he says most of it humorously. And bluntly. (Confidentially, he stings.)

No one has *ever* accused Corcoran of being shy. Critics might say he's shy a few marbles. But fans say he's marblous. He has a sharp eye (but no Shar-Pei), a sharp tongue and a sharp sense of humor.

John sharpened his critical powers while serving time in TV as an entertainment reporter and critic in Boston, Washington and Los Angeles. Now, his opinions appear in *ShopTalk*, an electronic newsletter about the broadcast industry. *ShopTalk* (www.tvspy.com) carries news about broadcast news—and buzz about the biz. It's e-mailed around the world by the S.I. Newhouse School of Public Communications at Syracuse University—free. In *ShopTalk*, Corcoran talks shop (but talks no Choctaw).

Cork calls himself Pesky Gadabout in *ShopTalk*, where he's a man of letters—about one a day. I wouldn't call him sarcastic. He's sarcaustic; he can burn your hide off. Or make you laugh your head off. Or chuckle and chortle. Or snicker and snort (no, not like a cokehead). Or mutter in anger. Or shudder in dismay. Whatever Cork makes you do, he won't make you drowsy or put you to sleep.

The book's table of contents should be called a table of *dis-*contents. Cork even takes a poke at my friends at the Radio-Television News Directors Association, and good friends they are. But Cork is uninhibited, unintimidated and unstoppable. Not to mention unleaded, unlicensed and undercapitalized.

So here he is, uncorked.

Forward!

# Give It Up For . . .

This is a partial list of those I'd like to thank for their contributions to this book, listed alphabetically by height, so no one will get his or her nose out of joint.

**Aunt Mary:** For underwriting the project. I'll miss you, especially your laughter.

**Dotty Corcoran:** My wonderful wife and the nicest person I know, for her patience.

**Andrew Corcoran:** For laughing at the right times, the encouragement and the help.

**John H. Corcoran III:** Who, during the dark times, wrote, "I'm proud that you've taken risks and followed your heart."

**Lt. Col. John H. Corcoran:** A brave man and good father who fought a war so people like me could write what we want to.

**Peggy G. Corcoran:** Mom, the kids turned out great.

**Devon Freeny:** If all editors were as skilled and easy to work with as this guy, writers would have much less to bitch about.

**Agnes Birnbaum:** My agent, who said not to call the book *Telebitchin'*, as I'd suggested, because it might scare off the big chains. I love her optimism.

**Merv Block:** For launching the project, for the encouragement and advice.

**'Becca Pullease:** For the encouragement and the compliments.

**Dave Gross:** For the friendship and support.

**Dana Hersey:** For the dinners, the friendship, the laughs and letting me do his radio show.

**Don Fitzpatrick:** For letting me rant on *ShopTalk*.

**Jack Limpert:** For giving me my first big writing break.

**Bob Shaw:** For the friendship and support.

**Michael Hirsh:** For the friendship and encouragement.

**Sam Zelman:** For my first TV job.

**Carole Cooper:** My former TV agent. For keeping me in the TV dodge long enough to learn enough to write a book about it. Don't blame her for my opinions.

**Correspondents on *ShopTalk*:** Both the encouraging and discouraging ones.

Also: **Bob Henry, Laura Carter, Wake-mon, Jocko, Jerry Dunphy, Tuna, Gavin, Habib, Mr. Know-It-All, Nurse Nancy, Dr. Doctor, Cassie** and, of course, **Oprah**.

And put your hands together for **Emmylou, Lyle, Oscar, Count, Louie, Pachelbel, Indigenous** and **Rhino's Doowop Box** for providing the soundtrack while I wrote.

# Author's Introduction

Hi. I'm the author, and this is my introduction. I'm writing this introduction because it's required by law.

I wanted to call this epic *A Book about the Business*, because everyone I've met in my career in TV has said, "You know, Larry, someday I'm gonna write a book about the business." My standard response was always the same: "My name isn't Larry and where'd you get that tie, guess somebody's weight?"

Then it struck me. Maybe *I* should write a book about the business and maybe even change my name to Larry. Then I said, whoa, one step at a time, big guy. So this is my book.

If you have already purchased the book, congratulations. A couple of those bucks go to me. The rest go to the publisher, the printer, the boys in the back room, to my lovely agent, Agnes Birnbaum, and to a guy named Vinnie, whom you don't want to know about, trust me.

So, if you've already made your purchase, you can skip over the rest of this crap and move on to the good stuff.

If you are standing in a bookstore thumbing through the book, trying to decide whether to buy it, let me make it easy for you: Pony up the purchase price, Sparky. This one is worth it.

If you're a reviewer, your brand new Buick is in the driveway.

An Author's Introduction is designed to tell you what you are about to read, and what gives the author the right to pose as such a big-deal expert that anyone should pay attention to what he thinks, anyway.

Most of these essays, satires, parodies, rants, fake speeches and letters use humor to make a point. I'd say some are funny as hell, except it's classier, I've been told, to let the reader discover that. On the other hand, screw class; I'm writing about TV news. Mostly. Because I have a mind like a steel trap—albeit one whose latches rusted out years ago—I also take a few shots at O.J., another odd Palm Beach vote, people who chew with their mouths open, and hucksters of all shapes and sizes. But this book's primary subject is TV news in all its agonizing, maddening lunacy (and its occasional moments of glory).

There are serious points to be made about the sad state of TV news, and I include enough of those to add *gravitas* to this tome. That way, I can tell my peers I don't "just" write humor but am a serious writer who can also make a real difference in society today. Tee-hee.

Okay, let's deal with the "expert" issue. Sure, you could buy a book by a professional educator and get the school-learning approach to TV news. Or you could buy a book by someone currently in the business, like a Dan Rather or Bill O'Reilly, both of whom, incidentally, are clinically insane.*

I used to work in TV news, and despite the jacket photo, I was on air—"Talent," as it's generically known. I was in a job I used to describe as "snack bar operator on a B-1 bomber." That is, nice to have around, but not critical to the mission. For twenty-odd years—some odder than others—I was an entertainment reporter and critic at TV news stations in Boston, Los Angeles and Washington, D.C.

I am out of TV news now, and would not return at the point of a gun. This means I can and do speak the truth. Of course I've

---

*It has been brought to my attention that either Dan or Bill might choose to sue me for libel at this point for either inferring or implying—I get those terms confused—that they are "clinically insane," as if I've seen records and commitment papers and such. Let me note at this time that throughout the book, all libelous references are satirical and hence not libelous (Cork's "Catch-23"). I do hereby state that I know for a fact that Dan Rather is not clinically insane, and that O'Reilly cannot be proven to be clinically insane, because his medical records were burned by Rupert Murdoch and David Duchovny.

got a bad memory, so if I've gotten a fact or two wrong, I apologize. These inaccuracies will be carefully removed and replaced by brand new inaccuracies in future printings and the movie version.

But then, what is "inaccuracy" anyway? Let's split the word up. First there's "accuracy," which means "having qualities of accurateness." Then there's "in," which means "inside or within boundaries of." Thus inaccuracy means "within the boundaries of accurateness." Hence, just as flammable and inflammable mean roughly the same thing, so too do "accuracy" and "inaccuracy," in my book. And this *is* my book, so I get to make the rules. Anybody want some gum?

Also, since I'm neither scholar nor practicing newsman, I can make key points using anecdotal evidence, fudged statistics and just plain lies, let the devil take the hindmost. I think you'll be amazed that with those sloppy standards, I'm so frequently dead on-target. I know I am.

This book includes some letters—mostly rewritten to protect the guilty—that were originally sent under the *nom de guerre* "Pesky Gadabout, Los Angeles & the World." These appeared in the broadcasting newsletter *ShopTalk* (www.tvspy.com), read in every television newsroom on earth. It's edited by the legendary Don Fitzpatrick, who likes my stuff, but don't hold that against him.

Enter a respected author and journalist named Merv Block. Merv kept pestering the publisher of Bonus Books, Aaron Cohodes, by sending him copies of my letters that ran in *ShopTalk*. Aaron finally asked me if I'd like to write a book. I said yes, and he sent me an advance that would choke a . . . well, maybe a minnow.

That's pretty smart on his part. See, since I don't have a Hillary-type advance, I've been forced to make this book good because if people don't buy it, I don't get paid. (Another reason to buy it? So lil' Timmy gets that operation he's always wanted.)

There are 77 pieces in all, including tips to help you get into or remain in the business, in case, y'know, you're nuts.

I've included a transcript of "The News Director's After-Sweeps Speech," which those knowledgeable in humor will recognize as an homage to Robert Benchley's fabled "The Treasurer's Report." (Benchley's grandson Peter wrote that book about the big fish.)

So what am I? Am I some embittered old cynic who can't stand the business he's no longer in and writes merely to get even for his miserable little career and all the mistreatment that he wrongly blames on others? Well sure, but there's much, much more.

I've got nice things to say, too. Read "I Really Should Give Jim Clark a Call" if you want to find out, in a nutshell, what I think is right with TV. And incidentally, if you know Jim's phone number, send it to me. I've misplaced it.

And believe me when I say I don't hate TV news. What I gripe about may be called TV news, but it ain't really. I just point that out. It's somebody else's job to fix it.

Okay, pal, this isn't a library, it's a bookstore. So before the clerk comes over and gives you grief, take the book to the register, buy it, read it, and tell your friends to go out and buy it. (No lending. You *know* that deadbeat will never return it.)

John Corcoran
*Casa Calabasas*
August 2001


(Martha: Slap some more false sincerity crap into this and send it on to the publisher. And bring me another martini, really dry this time.)

# The Shortest TV Newscast of the 21st Century

## Odd Observations of TV News

# The Shortest TV Newscast of the 21st Century
## A Transcript

Good Evening. I'm Gus Bivona. Tonight's news will be very short. The rest of our exclusive Live, Local and Late-Breaking Eyewitness Action Team Coverage Cam News Squad™ has been sent home.

We have no graphic footage of a parent's worst nightmare. There were no shocking crimes in a once-peaceful neighborhood. No neighbor described a lone gunman as "a quiet boy who never caused nobody no trouble."

None of our reporters are standing by live in the dark where a mile away and an hour ago something happened.

Nothing went wrong, terribly wrong, and no criminals were caught in the act, live on tape.

We have no exclusive reports, breaking news or live updates. SkyChopperCamSwiftwhirlyEyebird™ is on the ground.

No fires rage out of control. Flames are not leaping hundreds of feet into the air

There are no ominous developments.

There are no shocking turnabouts.

In weather news, there is no golf-ball size hail, no raging torrents, no white stuff headed our way. I will not laughingly turn to Wacky Wally on Weather and blame him for the rain.

We are not keeping our eyes on systems expected to unexpectedly intensify. There is no storm surge, so we are not, repeat, not on storm watch. Our StormCenter is closed. StormCam is turned off.

In sports, no record-setting contracts were signed, no one went to jail, no athlete spat on a five year old girl, no coach was punched, no one is holding out for more money and there is no crippling strike threatening to bring baseball/football/basketball/hockey to its knees.

At the end of this newscast we usually offer you an upbeat story. However, no cat is currently suckling a litter of baby pigs their mother rejected. No adorable endangered species cub made her public debut at the zoo. No freckle-faced teen Samaritan returned a missing bag of cash.

In short, there was no news today. At all. None.

My advice? Turn off your TV and read a book.

Good night, and remember: if it happened here, it's news to us.

# Can't Find the Sleaze? Import Some!

Now that sweeps is over (are over? am over?), and while all the data isn't in yet (aren't in yet? ain't in yet?), I've taken crayon in hand to draw some preliminary misleading conclusions. Once the data am all in, it will be possible to form permanent misleading conclusions backed by, uh, well . . . all that data.

First, let me reiterate, as I have iterated so many times before: data, research and statistics am what's wrong with TV. Not to mention, they is old-fashioned, unhip and no longer viable in this youthful-demographic-that-advertisers-covet era. Therefore, *quod est castrato*, I continue my quest to support conclusions only with anecdotal evidence.

For you latecomers, here's how anecdotal evidence works. Instead of proving a thesis based on mountains of indisputable, replicable evidence, you just come up with any old conclusion, harebrained or otherwise, then find an entertaining story to support your point of view. It saves a lot of time, effort and blue ribbon commissions. If that doesn't convince someone, just talk louder than the guy you're arguing with. If *that* doesn't work, hit him over the head with a folding chair.

Anecdotal evidence is right more often than not, and I have anecdotal evidence to prove that. Specifically, I'm getting fewer scornful e-mails and cackles of electronic laughter each time I open my piehole.

This brings me to the point at hand. And while we're at it, I'll thank you not to point at my hand. I'm a busy man, I rarely have time for a manicure and I have feelings, you know. But enough about me; on to my thesis.

Here in the greater Los Angeles area, as in most other places, local newscasts exist to convey ratings numbers only and not actual news; hence local newscasts are mostly crap.

Every sweeps, there are fresh examples to anecdotally confirm this assertion. For instance, take one story that appeared on a local newscast. (In the interests of fair play, and because so many other stations are also guilty, I won't report what network it was. For identification purposes only, the initials are NBC.)

I'd been watching *Law & Order*, which I tune in frequently because (a) it's intelligent, challenging and suspenseful entertainment, (b) it's on 23 times a day in reruns and (c) I want to see if Jerry Orbach's teeth have gotten their own series yet.

I remember it was a season ender and they were losing yet another cast member. *Law & Order* loses more cast members than *Survivor*. I recall weeping copiously over Benjamin Bratt's departure to pursue other opportunities and sleep with Julia Roberts. I ask you, whose mug would you rather stare at, Pretty Woman's or Sam Waterston's?

Then came the local 11 o'clock news. I have sympathy for the producers of these fast-paced programs. I know putting together what is laughingly referred to as a "half-hour newscast" ain't easy. What with budgeting time for the first block slaughter *d'jour*, wacky weather, the Evelyn Wood Speed-Reading Sports Scores, Mandatory Anchor Natterchat, commercials and plugs for tomorrow's "Can Implants Think?" sweeps special, there's maybe a three-minute newshole left to cram in the rest. If an anchor sneezes, it's cut to the kicker, and you're out the door.

Yet the newscast in question managed to find time for a two-minute-ish story about vice cops allegedly getting their batons waxed by the very masseuses they were supposedly investigating. According to claims by one of the magic-fingered ladies, cops were making four or more trips per masseuse to handle the evidence. It was only after they'd put their nightstick back in the holster that they broke the news to the ladies that they were headed to the pokey.

Video for the story consisted of blurry pictures of official documents and B-roll of a bikinied woman giving a massage so innocent it wouldn't raise eyebrows, suspicions or anything else. You couldn't tell if she was rubbing a man's back, a woman's calf or a leg of lamb.

Were there charges brought against these cops? Nope. Arrests? None mentioned. Celebrities or politicos involved? Not a one. Certainly, television news has an obligation to work for the common good, and one way is pointing out potential nefarious-ness before it gets out of, uh, hand.

However, as the embarrassed reporter fronting the piece in the studio noted, the events happened not in the Greater Los Angeles area, the Left Coast nor even the left half of the country. It was near Chicago. The one in Illinois.

Anecdotal conclusion: Sleaze in sweeps ain't going away. And if you wonder why the Profession Formerly Known as News now gets less respect than used car dealers, you need look no further than this ratings-driven non-event.

# Local News around the Land, Part 1
## Albuperky Glows for the Glodeo

*In the fall of 2000 I was a travelin' fool. The Missus and I took a long-postponed three-and-one-half-week train and car trip around the U.S. of A. A week after we returned, we hopped in the Hupmobile and scurried on up the California coast to Avila Beach, in central California. This vacation was designed to help us recover from our earlier vacation.*

*We stayed in a time-share, relaxed and visited nearby tourist attractions and beaches. My favorite was Pismo Beach, where Dotty and I walked hand in hand looking for seashells and trying not to step in the Pismo.*

*Whenever I could figure out the remote, I'd flip on the telly and catch a little local news. Based on this determinedly unscientific and anecdotal—hence pretty much dead-on—methodology, here is an update on the status of local news in America—spread out in four, easy, bite-size chunks in this section.*

**Albuquerque, New Mexico:** Or should we say Albu*perky*, New Mexico. Very, *very* perky newscasts for the Albuquerque and Santa Fe areas. Of course, it was the night before the big annual Santa Fe Hot Air Balloon Festival, which may have accounted for all the hot air. But I kid. With love.

Naturally, everyone led the news with the hot air balloons. The hot air live shots were from something called the "Glodeo

Festival," where a host of hot air balloons were tied down and lit up before floating out of town the next day. Sounds like a visit from my Uncle Phil.

"Glodeo" comes from combining the words "Glow" and "Rodeo." Had they also incorporated the word "balloon," it might have been named the "Blowdeo Festival."

It all appeared quite colorful on my 13" motel room TV. A perky reporter, standing in front of hundreds of perky balloons beginning to glow against the dark night, noted: "You can feel the heat as hundreds of balloons begin to glow against the dark night." When her live shot was over, she perkily returned to studio with a "Back to you-all."

The second lead story, a natural enough tie-in to the big hot air balloon story, was the next day's weather. This was part of team coverage of the recent, very heavy rains in the vicinity. The Perkycasters were all over that story.

Later, there was crime news:

"Our Action Seven network has been following this story," an anchor intoned. The story, about a missing woman and blood found in her home, included a weeping relative and was very unperky.

Another station had an item about an expensive government study done to see if there was too much arsenic in the local water. Arsenic in the local water is not good. One anchor wondered if the study was worth the money it cost to conduct. He said people wanted to make sure "all that money doesn't go down the drain." This is a pun. Newswriters love puns. Puns are referred to as the lowest form of humor. Some would argue it's a rare pun that even qualifies as "humor." Like Albuperky.

The reporter on the arsenic story was "Live!" of course. The consultants who determine what goes on the news *love* live shots as much as newswriters love puns. Thus the reporter was standing in front of a darkened building somewhere in downtown Albuquerque. This is known as a "Black Hole" live shot, since there is no one and nothing visible in the background that adds anything worthwhile to the shot. Perhaps they should have been at the Glodeo, too.

Ten minutes or so into the newscast, one station announced results of their "Exclusive" dot-com poll asking "whether or not the U.S. should stay in the Middle East." The results were 50-50. TV news is enamored of these kinds of dot-com surveys designed to increase viewership by getting people to leave their TVs and turn on their computers. Since local news ratings are down, the likelihood is that after voting, the former viewers surf for porn instead of dialing back to watch Wacky Wally on Weather.

One station *really* wanted you to know when it was updating a story. So it ran a slickly produced full-screen videotape of ambulances and newschoppers, complete with whooping sirens and whopping rotor blades. If you weren't looking at the TV, you might think you were missing a story about a helicopter crashing into an ambulance, but then, that might have been the idea.

Another station did a nice story about rudeness, noting that incivility may result in illness among the uncivil, which hardly seems like enough punishment.

Another had something called "SkyWarn" weather, which included the exclusive SkyWarn Forecast, and lots of neato SkyWarn Graphics. I really like the term "SkyWarn." It makes me want to go to the store and buy plywood for the windows and a six-week supply of canned beets.

The same station showed men riding bicycles, teasing an upcoming sweeps series with the ominous warning: "Get off that bike before you ruin your sex life!" In the spirit of synergy, perhaps they'll use "SeatWarn" or "CrotchWatch" graphics for the series.

As this was a Friday night, there were a lot of high school sports to cover. One sports guy unashamedly begged for someone—anyone—to call in with a missing high school football result. I'll bet the regular call-in guy blew off the football game and went to the Glodeo.

# Hey! Who Turned
# Out the Lights?

*This piece was written the first week of May, 1999.*

As news weeks go, this one has been extraordinary. You can start with the ongoing "ethnic cleansing" in Kosovo. "Ethnic cleansing" is a former euphemism that's rocketed up the common-usage charts with a speed that would make Casey Kasem dizzy. I guess "slaughter of innocent civilians" just isn't catchy enough.

Then there was Columbine High School, an event that left a media accustomed to making ratings-ready mountains out of everyday molehills caught up in a Gibraltar of a story that needed no adornment.

Yet adorn it they did, with snazzy graphics, on-the scene anchors, portentous music, intrusive questions, relentless tear-baiting and video of the terrorized fleeing victims used as so much B-roll fodder.

Then came the tornadoes of May, a story of F-4 magnitude. The screen was filled with images of splintered homes and lives and comprehensive video coverage that would make C. B. DeMille proud.

Call me weird, and you wouldn't be the first, but picking the most lasting image was a slam-dunk. For me, it was watching a local Ken and Barbie anchor duo, slapped up on the national satellite feed, and resplendently garbed in matching blue denim jumpsuits. Who ordered *those* puppies? What, did they think they might have to parachute into the story? What news guru said, "That's right; we feel the people of the Midwest will be better served knowing their news team has the presence of mind in a crisis to put on cool-lookin' threads"?

Then there was last night. I was surfing over to watch the big Julia Roberts stunt-casting *Law 'n' Order* episode and caught the end of that new NBC tentpole, *The World's Most Amazing Exciting Death-Defying Incredible Unbelievable Scary, Weird or 'Sploding Stuff Show*.

One of their stories was about an elephant that accidentally sat on a man. Just following the old news adage: Man sits on elephant—not news; elephant sits on man—news. But wait, there's more! See, at the time of the sittage, the misfortunate man was positioned with his head aligned with the elephant's—how can I put this delicately?—excretory orifice. When the elephant plotzed, the lights went out for the guy and Dumbo was thinking, "Gee, I thought my prostate exam was *next* week."

Three thoughts occurred to me:

1. On Wednesday, May 5, 1999, the National Broadcasting Company chose to entertain America by showing a guy with his head up an elephant's ass.

2. If that's not a sign of the Apocalypse, it should be.

3. On the other hand, it would have been really cool if right afterward someone asked the guy if he would quit his job, and the guy answered, "What, and get out of show business?"

# Unconventional Convention Coverage

*During the Democratic Presidential Convention of 2000, I flicked on the TV a couple of times to see how the locals were doing.*

## Day One

I've been dial spinning through convention coverage both as a civic duty and because of a distinct shortage of new infomercials offered as counterprogramming. Some observations:

C-Span offers far and away the best coverage once the night's formal activities have ended. That's when everyone else cuts to a commercial or a Thumbsucker Roundtable. C-Span stays live as people mill about and schmooze for as long as it takes to re-rack the network's encore presentation of the House Subcommittee's Dysfunctional Subcouncil on Inappropriate Oversight Hearings. So we are treated to delegates renewing old acquaintances and asking one another which strip club has the best two-for-one lap dance.

But when it came to thorough, in-depth coverage of the convention, the best work—just as it was in Philadelphia with the Republicans—was done by the Peabody award–winning team coverage of "Indecision 2000." Under the sharply cracked whip of anchor Jon Stewart, the *Daily Show* reporters blew away network heavies, CNN warriors and the Tom Brokaw–led MSNBC team, who spent most the night asking one another, "Didn't we used to do this on NBC?"

15

*Daily Show* highlights included a report from a Staples store (not the Staples Center that was the site of the convention), some on-air movie auditions by correspondents and, best of all, a creepy focus group.

Huzzah, *Daily Show*. Huzzah, Jon Stewart. Huzzah, all you huzzahworthy reporters and writers.

Local stations' news coverage of the convention "riots" varied. In L.A., many reporters have more riot experience than the cops. However, coverage today consisted mostly of sweating field reporters saying, "Thanks for asking me if the rioters a mile away are chewing Sen-Sen and wearing mismatched socks, Mr. Smug, Fat-Cat Overpaid Anchor sitting in a nice cool Skybox, too lazy to pick up the phone and find out for yourself," or words to that effect.

# Day Two

Didn't watch. Spent entire day working on my origami.

# Day Three

Watched the local news coverage of the threatened riots outside the Democratic Convention Wednesday. The riot ended up a big fizzle in the 100-degree heat, broke up early and everyone got home in time to catch the CBS masterpiece *Big Brother*. Here's an account. (All times and quotes approximate.)

**5:15 P.M.** KNBC anchor, perhaps in a fit of nostalgia for the Rodney King riots, refers wistfully to the previous night's lack of action outside the Staples Center: "Last night was maybe the lull before the storm."

**5:17 P.M.** KABC street reporter: "The violence seems to be increasing. We have to say this. Some are putting on masks and picking up rocks." Some gas masks are observed. No rocks are seen or thrown. Lots of sweaty people and cops.

**5:20 P.M.** A KABC anchor says: "We see people holding hands, very reminiscent of the 60s." I'm afraid she'll break into a quick chorus of Kumbaya.

**5:21–5:34 P.M.** Lots of milling, but still no rocks, little action, except on taped replays of earlier skirmishes. Some of these are irresponsibly shown without "taped earlier" bug. Several reporters refer ominously to "anarchists" disappearing under a hand-held "tent." No one suggests it might be to get out of the heat.

**5:35 P.M.** KNBC street reporter David Cruz has the best idea of the day when he starts grabbing bemasked anarchists and asking them just what is going on. The odd part is that to this point I've seen no other reporters doing this.

"Why are you wearing a mask?" Cruz asks a guy with a bandanna over his piehole. "I'm against corporate media," the protester says, lowering his mask and looking right into the corporate media camera. "We want you to tell us the news we really want."

A sweaty radical says he is there to protest "gross over-exaggeration of the city." Well, it *is* 100 degrees out.

**5:40 P.M.** KNBC anchors, perhaps feeling neglected, grab it back from Cruz, and soon one is grilling L.A.'s Republican mayor Richard Riordan in the convention hall: "Say, didn't I see you riding your bike today?" The mayor cracks under the grilling and admits that yes, indeed, that very morning he'd ridden the 15-mile trek from his Beverly Hills home to the eatery he owns. Hizzonor then proceeds to plug his eatery.

**5:41 P.M.** Moving in for the kill, the anchor unleashes another haymaker: "What is it like to hang with all those Democrats?" Riordan responds that fellow Republican Arnold Schwarzenegger is also on hand. "You know what?" the anchor says. "With Arnold, you could probably take 'em." The mayor retorts, "You're wonderful." No mention of protesters with rocks, or why we're watching this lovefest instead of reporter Cruz, who was interrupted interviewing actual protesters.

**5:45 P.M.** The mayor is now over at KABC-TV's convention booth, where he gets in another plug for his restaurant. So far the Republican restaurateur/mayor has gotten more air time than the Democrats.

**5:46 P.M.** Outside, another protester tells KNBC's Cruz he's protesting "the use of man's greater future."

But the protest has begun to break up. No rocks to be seen. Someone says the police on their bullhorns are addressing the protesters as "ladies and gentlemen." The tension oozes out like, like an oozing tension thing. (It's just too hot for metaphors or similes.)

**5:50 P.M.** KCBS, "The Station of the People," has snagged a dispirited protester: "It's like everyone is looking for their 15 minutes of fame. The leaders have no idea of what they want to do. Everything has gone haywire. it makes you miss the way protests used to be."

**6:00 P.M.** In the studio, KCBS co-anchors Jonathan Elias and Ann Martin toss it to themselves as the five o'clock news ends and the six o'clock news, which they are also anchoring this night, begins.

The speeches inside the Staples Center are about to begin, the protesters are heading home, and for the first time tonight, I spot a rock. Actually, *the* Rock. The same wrestling musclehead who graced the Republican podium is wandering around the floor of the Democratic Convention with the lovely Chyna, who somehow got past the silicone detector. Mayor Riordon is nowhere to be seen, apparently having pedaled home.

Outside, the anarchists, like the Martians in *War of the Worlds*, have been done in by an environment they can't tolerate. Their biggest mistake? Wearing L.A.-fashionable black-on-black outfits outdoors in the 100-degree weather. By prime time, they're too pooped to pop, and head home to Seattle, looking for a latte or a Starbucks to bomb.

Many of the local newsies, forged in the steel of the Rodney King riots, have played the scene like a band of out-of-condition ballplayers back in camp from too long an off-season. Others, especially Cruz, are in mid-season shape.

# Local News around the Land, Part 2
## The Plain in Maine
## Doesn't Strain the Brain

**Kennebunkport, Maine:** I watched a newscast while staying in the li'l seaside village of Kennebunkport, location of many lobstermen and ex-President George non-Dubya Bush's summer home. This was shortly before Halloween.

The stations I watched were in nearby Portland. The first thing I noticed was that Portland anchors were considerably less perky than the bunch in New Mexico. Their outfits tended more toward serious, adult clothing, dark wools and sensible accessories, not earth tones. The men wore serious ties on serious shirts. The women tended toward navy blues and sensible blouses.

There were no glowing hot air balloons in Portland this 37-degree day. I did find a corpse, an arrestee, an injured infant, some missing Mavericks and politicians running for office, however.

The stories tended to be more serious overall—is it possible consultants have been banned in the state? There were plenty of gee-whiz graphics and the requisite live shots, however, so probably not. There was a fresh murder. A child abuse story. An item about a prescription drug law challenge. There was an update on the presidential race. Notice was given that former Secretary of State Henry Kissinger had been hospitalized.

After fifteen minutes or so of serious news, two serious anchors lightened up at the end of the "A" block. After a story about the merger of two large dot-com companies, the male anchor said "w-w-w-dot-*bucks*."

This drew a smile from his co-anchor, who would look at home running an upscale souvenir shop in Kennebunkport.

At six, a twirl of the dial informed me that all three stations were leading with the stabbing death and arrest. Everybody was live at the scene. Everyone informed us the men had been good friends, and the stabbing took place at 4:45 A.M., apparently after a night of drinking.

This segued nicely into the second lead on all three stations, a battered baby story. Not five minutes into the first block and we had a corpse and a battered infant. So much for escaping the big city.

I decided to stick with the anchor team of Doug Rafferty and Kim Block on Channel 13. I felt at home with them. They fit their skin well. I wouldn't mind having them over for cocktails. I suspect that beneath their serious Maine exteriors may beat a pair of playful hearts. I think Doug would be a scotch drinker who, after several rounds of Johnnie Walker Black, would regale you with funny stories all night. Kim appeared to be the kind of good neighbor who would cheerfully lend you a loaf of bread. I think she drinks a white Zinfandel and has invested her money wisely.

Another reason I stuck with this station is they teased a story I actually wanted to watch. The story was re-teased each break until the end of the newscast, where it served as the kicker. According to the tease, the country/rock band the Mavericks were in Portland. I'm a big fan of the Mavericks.

But first there was a serious, well-produced package about two candidates running for a seat in Congress. I have rarely seen such a story told in such depth in Los Angeles.

Dave Stanford, the weatherman, was no Wacky Wally. Balding, solid, serious, he wore a dark, double-breasted suit. His approach to weather in this land where weather matters was properly respectful. There were no surf reports.

Barbara Barr did sports. She was open and appealing, a solid citizen, and she could fit in with the perky bunch in Albuquerque. Her lead was local high school sports, including soccer. She followed with a package about the Maine University Bears hockey team.

Finally, it was time for our visit with the Mavericks, and an old, familiar news-watching feeling reappeared. I'd been had. I had been enticed by false pretense, which I guess is pretty much what a news tease is supposed to do.

Turns out it wasn't the Mavericks after all. In fact, it was only 25 percent of their core membership. The Mavericks did not come to Portland to play. It seems one of their backup members, a member of the horn section, had matriculated at a local high school. He talked one of the "real" Mavericks, bassist Rob Reynolds, into accompanying him on a visit to his old high school. There they both encouraged the kids, musicians particularly, to follow their dreams, to work hard and practice, man, practice. That way, you too may get to play with the Mavericks, and drag one of them back to your high school to impress the chicks with how cool you've become.

I checked my notes, and they were inconclusive as to whether the teases had promised that all the Mavericks would be on the news. But then, as another songwriter said in another context, a man hears what he wants to hear.

There was another surprise left on this newscast, and it confirmed why I like this anchor team. After the tossback, Doug said, with some sense of earnestness, "Yeah, well, it's great what they are doing with those kids and stuff, going to the schools and teaching them. . . ." He then paused and laughed what might be interpreted as a scoffing laugh, all anchor pretense gone for an instant. He turned to his co-anchor and said, "That's not like us when we go to Career Day and say, 'Don't do *this!*'"

*This*, of course, is what Doug and Kim had been doing for the past hour. Doug had let us inside that reserved Maine-ish exterior for a heavy dose of honesty.

# *Dateline* Gets One
# Oh So Right

I stumbled onto a story on *Dateline* the other night. I watch *Dateline* when I think of it, especially when it's not opposite *The Sopranos* or my favorite Discovery Channel program, *Inside Forensic Insects*. I like to catch pieces by my former co-worker and pal Josh Mankiewicz and to see whether Stone Phillips's face has grown an expression yet. (Someone told me—or perhaps I dreamed it—that Phillips is a riot off camera, "pantsing" the crew and starting water balloon fights.)

Instead of the usual fare, this night's single-topic *Dateline* brought me a lot more than I expected.

I picked up the Keith Morrison report in progress. It was about an American GI named Richard Luttrell, who had killed a North Vietnamese Army soldier in combat 34 years ago. The American had recovered a photo from the slain NVA, a photo of the soldier and his then–six-year-old daughter. The soldier was in uniform; the little girl stared straight out at the camera, as if she suspected the worst might happen.

The story followed the picture's journey from the jungles of Vietnam to the Vietnam Memorial in Washington, D.C., where Luttrell left it. "It was a final salute to him," Luttrell said, "He died fighting for what he believed in. And it was a way to honor and respect him."

The photo was gathered up and eventually used in a published book of items left by the Wall. We learned the man who had killed the father of the little girl was still haunted by the photograph.

And so he decided to try to find the daughter. He learned, through amazing coincidence, that the now-grown woman was still alive and living outside Hanoi. Luttrell, his wife, Morrison and his crew then journeyed to that little village, where Luttrell met the woman for the first time.

There one of those rare magical television moments happened. The two first stood awkwardly as Luttrell read, in halting Vietnamese, a statement he had prepared.

Then the woman broke down and they embraced, and soon he was crying, and I was, too. Thirty-four years before that moment, a trigger had been pulled, a soldier killed and a little girl's life changed forever. Now, with the guns silent, the man who had done his duty, this former enemy, was embraced by the daughter of the man he killed. And now and forever that once faceless enemy would be recognized as what he was— an individual and a father, and a man loved and missed by a little girl.

It showed just how good the medium of television news can be. It can convey genuine emotion with a clarity and reality unmatched by any other medium.

But its power and ability to move us has been undercut by overuse and misuse, by intentional manipulation of viewers' emotions, by preying on grief for profit.

We are inundated as never before by the banal and the manipulative use of grief and tears as just another tool of the television trade. From every five-and-dime reporter who has tear-jerked a bereaved relative because it "makes good television," to Barbara Walters trying to pull the saltwater out of Patsy Ramsey with her "Do you still dream of JonBenet?" question, the tube is awash with ratings-driven crocodile tears. The effect is numbing.

All this falsely obtained emotion detracts from the real tragedies, the true horrors of everyday life and uncommon events, diminishes the singularity of death and loss. To present such emotion should not be some TV sideshow run as a matter of course. It should be something the medium should do only from its heart, not from its research.

Like any drug, this daily intentional infliction of emotional distress lessens in impact after a while. A nation inured to tears and honest emotion is one that turns off its own.

The cure won't come from consultants or bottom-line management. It must come from the reporters and producers themselves who will have the courage and the class to not ask the question designed to break down a victim of loss, to not take the easy way out and to have the self-discipline and compassion to know when enough is enough.

# Scream Like a Howler Monkey

I tuned in to get a load of Joseph Lieberman on the eleven o'clock news here in Los Angeles the day he was announced as Democratic veep candidate. I figured L.A. would be all over the story. It's a company town, and the company is the Business of Show. And Lieberman has whacked Hollywood upside the head early and often for making dirty pictures. And violent pictures. Sounds like the lead story to me.

You want more? The man could have been one heartbeat away from the presidency. One heartbeat from turning Ahnold and Sly into pussycats. This was a man who strongly suggested that the entertainment industry restrain itself in portraying violence and sexuality on-tube and on-screen, and sent a chill through the Hollywood Hills.

Also, Senator Lieberman was the first Jewish man ever nominated for the vice presidency. He was among the first to point out the questionable morality of President Clinton's dalliances. That's news.

But instead of leading with the birth of a new era of politics, all three network affiliates led with a childbirth along one of L.A.'s ubiquitous freeways.

The healthy baby was delivered with help from its dad, who listened to instructions from the 911 baby-birthin' expert. But wait, there's more! We got screams! Yeah, baby! Everybody in TV Land got to hear the woman screaming in the background on the 911 tape. Even heard a screech from the kid, and later saw him swaddled in Mom's arms while she said, "He was a quiet boy, never caused nobody no trouble before."

Did Lieberman's selection follow? Nope. As long as we're talking roadside attractions, L.A., we have a small plane landing safely on a highway, and we have that automatic go-to-the-front-of-the-newscast item, a shooting of someone by someone else, somewhere else. Eventually, well into the first block, five minutes into the broadcast, the first station mentioned Senator Lieberman.

Why not sooner? Too dry, I'm guessing. If Lieberman had wept tears of joy, or screamed like a howler monkey, or said he was gay, or fondled his wife, or had given birth to an alien life form on camera, sure, that's a no-brainer lead. But mere politics? *Boorrrriiinnngg!* We're here to entertain the rubes, not inform them. They'll get their politics through the 30-second spots on our station. And Lord, don't the money roll in.

I know I'm spitting against the windbags. Marketing boys and bottom liners are increasingly the ones making the calls in TV "news." But I'm old enough to remember when news had a sense of responsibility, and a sense of obligation to inform the public on important issues, and not just feed their emotions so they'll buy your soap.

I've been accused of whining too much about the local news scene. I'd stop whining about the atrocities of L.A.'s local news if they just admit they're ratings and bottom-line driven, consultant-infected, journalistically unsound, video-trumps-words, emotion-trumps-thought, amoral devices designed to earn money, and will not let important news get in their way. And yes, I know they do good stuff, too. Just not enough.

Perhaps we could rename these former newscasts to reflect their actual content. Of course we'd have to run the new name through consultants and the focus group galvanic fandango, but when has that ever stopped anything in TV?

Here's my title idea:

*The Thrills 'n' Chills, Nifty Video, Car Chase If We Got 'em, Shoot-'em-up Emotioncast, Presented By Perky People Who Laugh and Cry Just Like You, Plus Sports and Wacky Wally on Weather Show.*

I say it's time to drop the pretense and cut the umbilical to Edward R. and Severeid and Chet and David and Walter and other genuine journalists.

Just a thought, or, more precisely, a delusional hallucination.

# Local News around the Land, Part 3
## We Got the Skinny on Weather, by God

**New Orleans:** We had only a day and a half in New Orleans. I did very little TV watching here, preferring instead to eat myself sick. I did notice the night we arrived that WDSU had some really nifty-sounding weather gizmos. There was a "Super Doppler Storm Center," a "Storm Scan" and something called "Futurecast."

This is great stuff. I cannot imagine watching anything other than this station for fear I might miss some Super Doppler Futurecasted Storm Scan cloud formation. If I owned a competing station in New Orleans, I think I would just tell my news director to suggest everyone tune to WDSU during the weather segment, and dip to black for five minutes. What's the use?

One station has tried to one-up WDSU by bringing in the Ultimate Weather Consultant. Their weather block is sponsored by the Faith Church of New Orleans. I have never heard nor read of a religious faith sponsoring a weather forecast before. I half expected to hear something like "Partly cloudy tomorrow, with little chance of rain, praise Jesus."

Everyone, including Storm Scan Watch and the GodCast, has the same prediction—a partly cloudy tomorrow. This is fine; my wife and I will be doing the tourist bit.

The next morning starts as predicted. The sun peaks in and out of clouds. It is humid but not too hot. We take a morning bus tour, eat some beignets—which are to your arteries what hairballs

31

are to your plumbing, only considerably tastier. Then the clouds chase away the last of the sunshine, and it rains. It rains most of the rest of the afternoon, a steady though not heavy downpour that leaves us damp but not soaked.

So much for satellites and sacred connections. It is, we learn that night, the first rain in the Crescent City in six weeks.

# Tan Lines and Facial Hair:
# A Beach Story

Here's one of my all-time favorite local news teases. The story was about women suffering the heartbreak of unwanted facial hair. The news item itself is not at issue. Far be it from me to mock the pain and embarrassment of women who face the mirror each morning with a caterpillar on their lip. And what woman wants to bump into Mr. Right and have him ask, "Excuse me, buddy, where's the men's room?"

I likewise sympathize with the challenge of finding appropriate video for a tease of this nature. No viewer wants to dine while watching Dr. Tweez-a-Lot depilate a hairball in a party dress. Viewers' appetites are battered enough from those irritable bladder ads that already grace the dinner hour. And nothing like live childbirth on *Good Morning America* to take the edge off your morning Mueslix.

The station could simply have shown women from behind and let viewers assume they had a Sherwood Forest thing going on 'round front, but even I know that's not good television.

So, what do you think the boys in marketing came up with? Are you sure you want to stick with that answer? Would you like to consult anyone? Here we go: The tease video consisted of women in bikinis. Beautiful women in small bikinis, lying on the beach. The women displayed admirable endowments but, alas, no visible facial hair nor other obvious connection to the story in question.

# Such Terror. Such Agony.
# Such Heartache. Such Crud.

I watched a couple of hours' coverage by Los Angeles stations of the killing of two kids and wounding of others by a 14-year-old with problems and a gun. As it so happened, it was also a very rainy day in L.A., which is always a huge story.

Bearing in mind that the former was a fast-breaking story, and the kind of blood and emotionalism that TV news loves, it still reached embarrassing levels of hackneyed writing. There were more clichés in evidence than uh, well, than you could shake a stick at.

I wondered if it might be possible to assemble the clichés into one big, clichéd news story, using the phrases uttered on the newscasts I'd listened to. Piece of cake, with plenty left over.

While a certain amount of familiar language will be used under times of stress and fast-breaking news, it amazes me how many of these words and phrases were hysterical, melodramatic and hyperbolic.

*(Phrases heard on the air are in **boldface**.)*
**It happened again. Gunfire rang out** on a **Monday that no one will forget** while **panic gripped a Southern California high school** during **a random act of rage**. There **was terror inside a high school** as a **sleepy Monday morning turned into a bloodbath** and **gunfire shattered another community** that **won't be the same again.**

35

Keep it right here; we'll have **live team coverage** of more **deadly developments** in this **deadly rampage** that is **close to our own backyard** and **turns lives upside down.**

This raises all kinds of questions, so many unanswered questions. Why did it happen? Why today? Could it happen in *our* schools?

**To add to the horror, a nation is in shock** over this **deadly rampage today** as **emotions ran the gamut** and **gunfire shatters the innocence of youth.**

We're learning more about the suspect in **this tragic act of violence, terror and tragedy.**

In summary, **people try to make sense of this senseless act of violence** at yet another **scene of terror.** What else can we say but, **"Such terror. Such agony. Such heartache."** Back to you.

L.A. stations also noted that **we're on storm watch all night** because **it's gonna get a lot worse before it gets better.** And of course there was live team coverage of **the soggy Southland saturated with rain** and feeling **the force of Mother Nature.**

I do not mean to be callous to those who suffered greatly. But they deserve better than to be the victim of manipulative, titillating words and phrases that have emigrated from tabloids and dime novels into common television usage.

# Isn't That Reddy Kilowatt Driving That Truck?

I am typing this by candlelight on my ethanol-powered PC because I live in California, a state that is in the midst of a power crisis. It seems electricity was deregulated, and electric companies now have to buy power from Ohio, Sri Lanka and Texas at usurious rates that it can't pass along to customers. The extra money lands in the pockets of George W. Bush's campaign contributors, which is just a coincidence.

By golly, the utility companies are broke. We knew they were in trouble when eyewitnesses spotted industry bigwigs being driven to *public* golf courses in unwashed limos. Just last week, they laid off cartoon mascot Reddy Kilowatt.

By the time this is read, I assume the problem will be solved, the electricity will flow like water and we'll be able to toss toasters into the tub just for fun. (Hey, kids! Kidding! Don't do that with the toasters. It will either kill you or make your muffin mushy, and nobody likes a mushy muffin.)

But back when our darkest hour started, I dialed up the news to see how the locals were covering the crisis. A critical Public Utilities Commission meeting was taking place January 3, 2001— in emergency session—to raise electric rates.

The president of Edison is on the tube in commercials every night, just like the Ford guy when those Firestone tires started 'splodin'. Mr. Edison solemnly assures everyone it isn't his fault, and to think otherwise makes the public thankless bastards who don't appreciate the pain our beloved electric companies are in. He adds, "We all have to pull together," which, translated from corporate talk, means, "You schmucks will pay, not us."

The governor of the Great State of California is trying to come up with an answer that will keep the lights on and the citizenry from storming Sacramento. (Having the capitol in Sacramento now looks like a stroke of genius. Who the hell wants to storm Sacramento?) Apparently droughts in the upper Northwest have something to do with the crisis, but nobody's figured out a way to blame God.

It is far and away the biggest story in California. Has been for months. Won't go away soon. Affects everyone. Enormous consequences for personal quality of life and the statewide economy. *Huge* story.

I checked out all four ten o'clock newscasts on L.A. stations to see 'sup. (Hey man, I gotta confirm my street cred every so often.)

Sure enough, all four stations had the same lead story. Three of the four stations stayed with that lead story for *the entire first half hour* of their broadcast. Experts were brought in. Phoners went on the air. Reporters called in from reporter cars with breaking developments.

In time of crisis, no one can say that TV news in Los Angeles won't step up to the plate and turn over half their newscast to a single story.

The electrical crisis? Naaaaw. Truck chase. Guy blew by a weigh-station in a semi, and the police wanted to talk to him. He wouldn't pull over. So the cops followed him around the area. The "truck chase" was at legal speed limits, the guy stopped at stop signs and red lights, and he appeared to be driving safely at all times.

Before long, he was followed by a dozen police cars, police choppers and the media horde of whirlybirds. At least one reporter was in a chase car. At 10:30, the trucker drove into a truck marshaling yard and surrendered peacefully. All in all it was about as dangerous and thrill-seeking a chase as the Rose Bowl Parade.

Yet, perhaps in the hope he might run down some old lady like the guy in the previous chase had, the stations stuck with it—except KCOP, which might have been acting responsibly or saving a buck by keeping its chopper grounded. Not until the guy was in the squad car and headed off to the pokey did the other three stations resume normal broadcasting. One anchor reported that the trucker took a last puff from a butt before flipping it away and raising his hands as ordered by police.

Normally, I wax hysterical about such matters but I think the infinite broadcast universe will solve the problem soon. The Internet is already working on "all chase, all the time" coverage. It shouldn't be too long before one channel or another in the great gaping maw of cable goes to that format. (With "Greatest Chases and Blowed Up Cars" specials filling the time in between.)

So remember, it ain't news unless the TV says it's so.

# Local News around the Land, Part 4
## Everyone Dies in the "A" Block

**Central California (San Louis Obispo, Santa Barbara, etc.):**
The newscast is a slaughterhouse, a veritable pit of pain, suffering, explosions and death. The violence on the screen is such a contrast to the beautiful central California coast out the window.

In the course of a single newscast, one learns:

- A 72-year-old woman is dead in a hit-and-run accident. The police are seeking the owner of a Pontiac Fierro.
- A boat has exploded. The name of the boat is "Dynomite." The blast has been deemed suspicious. Name a boat "Dynomite" or a restaurant "Arson Fire," and you're just naturally gonna attract suspicion.
- A Santa Maria Albertson's grocery store was viciously attacked by a 78-year-old woman in an automobile. She claimed she didn't mean to do it.
- A 20-year-old cheerleader fell through a skylight.
- A student at the University of Michigan, who had, near as I could tell, no connection to central California, drank 20 shots of whiskey on his 21st birthday and will not be celebrating his 22nd birthday.
- A woman in Alabama was assaulted.
- There was a follow-up story on the scores of skiers burned to death in the Alps tunnel accident.
- Leah Rabin is dead.
- So are many more people killed in the Middle East.

And that's just the first block.

In the second block, the carnage pauses momentarily and there is a feature on Space Heater Safety Tips.

Included is this advice:

"Whatever you do, don't use a barbecue to heat your home. Why? Because the fumes it gives off will kill your family." I'm reminded of Dennis Miller's line, "Sometimes you've just got to thin the herd."

The male anchor for the massacre is okay, but I really like the female co-anchor. Her name is Rachel and she's well tanned. She has extremely, dazzlingly, toothpaste commercial–quality brilliant white teeth. She doesn't show them very often. But when she does, the effect is like a signalman's light blinking from a destroyer on a starless night.

It is uncommonly cold in the central coast.

"We are moving into the wild and wacky weather time, right?" Rachel blinks at us and her co-anchor.

"Not so wild and wacky," the co-anchor responds, not caught up in the spirit of her good humor. "Just cold."

So much for Happy Talk. They toss quickly to Wacky Steve on weather, catching him not at his weatherboard but taking a gulp of tea. Steve has the flu, but is soldiering on with a little help from some herbal tea. Steve understands the basic rule of TV news—you always come to work no matter how contagious you are. This both reassures management that you are truly indispensable and helps build resistance to new strains of flu among your co-workers.

# Summary

What did I learn during these glances at TV news from around the country? There are, of course some regionalisms left, but based on this anecdotal glimpse, the McDonaldization of TV news is about complete. The hands of consultants are everywhere, with familiar formats abounding—the same pacing, the same mindless anchor-chat, the relentless dependence on MOS interviews, the high story count, the team coverage of fluffy events and the ignoring of real issues.

Newscasts, once put together by journalists, are increasingly overseen by salesmen in news clothing, or that accumulation of hangers-on and failed wannabes who've dropped out of news and taken up consulting. There is little originality from area to area, just the same old crap served out of different cans.

# Some Kinda Plane with Lotsa People in It Crashed

I kept track of Los Angeles TV coverage of the January 2000 Alaska Airlines MD-83 crash—the good, the bad and the ugly. Without identifying reporters or anchors or the six stations I surfed, here's what viewers learned in a one-hour period shortly after the accident (5:15–6:15 P.M.):

> We think the flight number is 261. We're trying to get confirmation of this.
> —*Anchor, terrifying some, merely discomforting others.*
>
> We don't want to go in too close here, in case there are body parts.
> —*Chopper pilot to his onboard cameraman.*
>
> Careful. Oh, they told you to go in?
> —*Same chopper pilot to cameraman moments later, after cameraman zoomed in on debris, apparently on instructions from someone in control room.*
>
> The water temperature is warm. No problem with hypothermia.
> —*Station weathercaster, brought in for expertise.*
>
> The water is very cold, about 10 degrees below normal.
> —*Another station's weathercaster, brought in for expertise.*

First there was the Egyptair 737 that crashed . . .
—*Anchor, recounting recent air tragedies. (Egyptian
plane was a 767.)*

An MD-80 carries a cockpit crew of six individuals.
—*Anchor. (MD-80 has a cockpit crew of two
individuals. Cabin crew on this flight was three.)*

What caused the plane to fall from the sky is still very
much unknown.
—*Anchor, avoiding dreaded "only time will tell" cliché.*

An Alaska Airlines pilot I talked to who has flown that
route says the flight usually flies full, with 146 passengers.
—*Field reporter.*

The plane has a capacity of about 160 people.
—*Field reporter.*

An MD-80 can seat between 92 and 172 passengers.
—*Anchor.*

The plane was a Boeing 737 twin-jet airliner.
—*Anchor.*

It is either a Boeing 737 or an MD-80. We still don't
know how many aboard.
—*Anchor.*

Seattle confirms 65 passengers and five crew. FAA said the
plane was a 737. A Boeing spokesman says the company
was told by Alaska Airlines that the plane was an MD-80.
—*Anchor.*

We previously reported 65. [Our reporter] said it was 55
on board. Now Alaska says 85.
—*Anchor.*

The FAA has confirmed it is an MD-80, not a 737.
—*Anchor.*

The FAA is now saying the plane was an MD-83.
—*Anchor.*

The FAA reports this is not a 737 but an MD-80.
—*Anchor.*

If indeed it is a 737, that is the only problem, major problem that has been reported, they call it a hardover. The rudder would actuate to one side.
—*Chopper pilot, describing recent 737 crashes.*

The pilot had a chance of landing at other airports in that area. Point Magu. We are now moving from fact to speculation. The pilot evidently figured he could get back to LAX, which is what he requested. We don't know if the pilot declared a Mayday.
—*Anchor/pilot.*

It could have been an ae-EE-ler-on problem.
—*Anchor/non-pilot*

We've learned the water is about 400 feet deep . . .
—*Anchor.*

Deep-water rescue.
—*Co-anchor, showing knowledge of terminology and ignorance of situation.*

It might have been inverted or upside down.
—*Anchor.*

Belly up.
—*Co-anchor, clarifying for those who don't know what "inverted or upside down" means.*

What's significant about the plane being belly up? It could
mean there was a complete loss of the airline.
—*Field reporter.*

American Airlines officials are gathering relatives
—*Reporter at sister station in San Francisco.*

As with all airline tragedies, there's a sense of community.
—*Field reporter on a beach with lookyloos, ten miles
from the crash site.*

# The New
# News Rules

## A Look behind
## the Scenes

# The New
# News Rules

Here's a handy Clip 'n' Save list of local news stories in descending order of priority. Please post near the assignment desk.

- School shooting with deaths
- Major aircraft accident, local
- High-speed car chase, with accident or shootout
- Car chase, without accident or shootout
- Storm Watch*
- Closing or opening of, or protest against strip bar
- Celebrity stalker arrested, Madonna involved
- Celebrity stalker arrested, Madonna not involved
- Dead or missing child with photo of cute child
- Dead or missing child with photo of ugly child
- Drive-by or other gang-related shooting (less than 24 hours old)
- Dead non-gang teenager, or cute adult murdered or kidnapped
- Rapper shot, arrested, or with controversial new record
- Dead suburbanite, other than suicide, unless murder/suicide
- Local sports hero arrested for possession of controlled substance
- O.J. arrested again
- Pit bull attacks child
- Kitten up a tree (kicker only)

---

* Storm Watch: In most cities this means impending or actual blizzard, hurricane, tornado or other severe weather phenomenon. In Los Angeles, it's drizzle.

- Horse stuck in the mud
- Madonna pregnant again
- Nuclear warhead missing
- National espionage or corporate malfeasance
- Freeway accident, one killed*
- Bus drives off cliff in India, 50 or more killed or missing
- Ferry sinks in Philippines, 500 or more killed or missing
- Cockroach found in station manager's salad, salad bar operator arrested
- Robert Downey remanded, released or returned to jail
- Political figure (other than Clinton†) arrested for DUI
- Station reporter or GM arrested for DUI

---

\* Move up three slots per additional death.

† Bill Clinton involved, add ten slots.
  Hillary Clinton involved, add five slots (except New York).
  Roger Clinton involved, drop five slots.

# The Anchor Has Five Faces

Being a local TV anchor is not as easy as it looks. I'm sure many civilians think anchors have an easy life and are grossly overpaid, and would love to have their job. Not necessarily true. Local TV anchors have a lot to worry about, including a lot of people who know less than they do, who tell them what to do and then fire them.

Let's start with what you see on air. Anchors must look intelligent, friendly, approachable and dignified, and express a wide range of expressions—okay, five expressions.

Anchors have five separate and distinct faces to reveal to the audience at home:

**Anchor Face.** This is the noncommittal face on display at times when the other faces are inappropriate.

**Happy Face.** This is used when a pet squid is rescued from a sewer and returned safely to her crippled five-year-old owner.

**Sad Face.** This is used when someone's child was brutally murdered during a drive-by.

**Angry Face.** Useful for some great social indignity, such as when gas prices rise and the anchor has to pay an extra five spot to gas up the Lexus.

**Perplexed Face.** Anchor uses this for story where police have no clues as to whereabouts of missing heiress.

Newscasts always strive to end the show with an upbeat piece such as a horse rescued from a mud flow, an otter that's taken in a family of musk ox babies, or a parakeet who's friends with a porpoise. But in the stress of battle, sometimes the story flow doesn't quite work out.

Most critical is the ability to switch smoothly, appropriately and sometimes immediately from one Anchor Face to another, without appearing insincere, or like someone whose gumball machine is short a few gumballs.

An example: An anchor might be called upon to instantly transition from Sad Face to Happy Face when a producer follows up a piece on the death of 300 Filipinos with the story of a rescued pet.

> . . . it is the greatest loss of life on a Filipino ferry since last week's sinking. Meanwhile, today, good news for a local kitty. It looks like Mr. Whiskers used up most of his nine lives today, before rescuers . . .

Without a transition story to avoid a charley horse in your smiley muscles, there is only a split second between the gut-wrenching sadness Mr. Anchor must show for the ferry going down and his grin-like-a-loon glee that the pussycat survived.

Another thing an anchor must master that is harder than it appears is making the eye-contact shift from one camera to another. This move is planned, and cued by a stage manager or floor director. The floor director trains for this by watching old black-and-white newsreels of the flag guy trying to wigwag a crippled Navy Corsair onto the pitching deck of an aircraft carrier.

Here is another key anchoring skill: an anchor must look like she likes her co-anchor, even if he's a swine or is blowing garlic breath her way that could kill a rattlesnake. The anchor must learn to look attentively at the co-anchor as the co-anchor reads, occasionally turning to the camera, as if to include the bozos at home in the little conversation group. The anchor cannot look as if she can't wait to read her stuff, move her lips while she reads along, or count each word aloud to make sure she's getting her fair share of face time.

Anchors must be masters of chitchat. They must have the right phrase handy when their co-anchor or someone in the field speaks to them. Because of time constraints, they must have short summary phrases after field reports. An anchor must be able to pull out the following at a moment's notice:

- Thank you for that.
- Stay on top of it. In other news . . .
- I should say so.
- I should say not.
- Powerful story.
- Nice job.
- Our prayers are with them.
- Wasn't that the darlingest kitty/puppy/baby ever?
- Save some for me!
- I guess we can all count our blessings.
- Sad, sad. Tragic. Just very sad.
- We wish the mayor well during his latest incarceration.
- I thought that marriage would last.
- As long as they do it for the kids.
- As long as they don't do it in front of the kids.
- Ummmgh. Quite a sight!
- Give them my best.
- Amazing how they can be young and so smart.
- Soon she'll be after my job.
- Truly, it was a parent's worst nightmare.
- A happy day for us Dodger/Yankee/Cubs fans.

A lot has been made about anchor salaries. Especially in the major markets where a top man or woman can break the seven-figure barrier. (My salary once broke the seven-figure barrier, but I *hated* what they did with the decimal point.)

No one overpays an anchor out of sympathy. Anchors get what the market will bear. They are paid a lot because a successful anchor, one with the innate ability to be likable and authoritative and welcome in viewers homes, can mean millions of dollars in profits.

But why are they paid so well if the gig seems so easy? To understand why even overpaid TV people aren't really overpaid, consider this Jack Lemmon story.

I once interviewed Lemmon when he had a horrific cold. As luck would have it, we had faulty equipment, and I had to keep

Jack Lemmon waiting, sniffling and sneezing for a half hour before the interview could begin. I apologized profusely, and he told this story.

He once had a print reporter spend a day with him on the set of his latest movie. The reporter arrived at Lemmon's call time, 5 A.M. After makeup and costume Lemmon was ready for picture at 7 A.M. Oooops. Picture wasn't ready for Lemmon; would he wait a few minutes?

A few minutes turned into hours until an assistant director told Lemmon they were breaking for lunch.

By the time lunch was over, the sky had clouded over. There was a weather hold, so today's picture would match yesterday's.

By the time the clouds lifted, doubt set in about a scene. The screenwriter was giving it a quick polish. The quick polish lasted until the clouds were back, and at 6 P.M. Lemmon was told that was a wrap for the day and they'd see him same time the next. He'd shot exactly zero frames of film that day, and had spent all his time cooped up in his trailer.

The writer asked him, Doesn't that infuriate him?

"No," Lemmon said. "They pay me for this. The acting I do for free."

And so it is in television. The work, when it's right, is its own reward. You are paid for the crap you put up with.

That includes consultant boobery, bosses who make you paranoid, missed baseball games and parties, and the fact that to move up, you must usually uproot your family and move across the country.

They pay you for *that,* not the work.

Because anchors are now suffering from lowered pay and prestige, because they get canned as part of any new news director's self-preservation program, because they must pay alimony for one or two wives left behind, because they must dress well and drive a nice car in public, because everyone wants their job and their salary, they are compensated more than they seem to be worth.

If that's what you want to do, in spite of the warnings, take my advice and go with God.

# I'm Not Just
# Another Pretty Face

I ain't no Pretty Boy. Never have been. But I lasted nearly 20 years in the biz. Oh, I cut a presentable enough swath, but if I heard the word "hunk" tossed in my direction, it was usually in reference to something stuck in my beard. As I'm about half a recessive gene away from being too repulsive for television, I have empathy for people not pretty enough for the tube. After all, the Good Lord in His infinite wisdom and mercy decided there should be ugly people, and when it appeared there were too many ugly people, He invented plastic surgery. Now ugly people can become less ugly people. Some ugly people can even pretty themselves up enough to be on TV. Many have.

For instance, an otherwise ravishing beauty with a nose the size of a macaw's can have it carved down to a manageable size and go on to fame and fortune.

Likewise, a weak-chinned but buff dude can have the doc slap a slab of fake granite on his jaw bone, throw in a dimple and be an immediate babe magnet, and anchor material.

In different media, looks have varying importance. For instance, newspapering has traditionally been a province where looks don't matter one iota. A butt-ugly newsie who can delivery 500 well-crafted words under a crushing deadline has always been of immense importance to his employer. Editors don't think, "Big story? Better send the good-looking guy."

Authors, traditionally, have paid no concern to their looks. Hidden away in a windowless room, pounding out deathless prose, living on coffee and amphetamines, writers live a life that doesn't make for an attractive human. And except for the jacket photo—which can be faked—looks don't matter much. It has been a great relief to me to be able to let myself go as I wrote this book.

Radio? Until someone got the bright idea of pointing a TV camera at Howard Stern, this never was an issue. And Stern's no day at the beach. Imus? Well, Imus has a face with character. Rush Limbaugh? 'Nuff said. Dr. Laura? Forget the gay-bashing. Her TV show bombed because she's got a face for radio.

It's not that radio people are unattractive—far from it in some cases—but it just doesn't matter. In fact, the most attractive women tend to congregate around rock jocks.

Which brings us to TV and the Pretty Boy Syndrome. Lotsa pretty boys and knockout babes in TV. Some even have news chops.

Take Brian Williams. Williams is an anchorman/model/ whatever at MSNBC and NBC. He is serious on the news but scores comedically every time he does panel on a talk show. He's a rare combo-pack. Handsome, smart, witty, and quick with a jibe or a comeback.

Once, during the post–non-election crisis Brian appeared on Letterman, loopy from overwork. Williams, deadpan, pointed out to Dave that it's just possible former New York Mayor Ed Koch had become president over the weekend. Brian also noted his network was better than CNN because even if MSNBC lost *two* letters from its name, it would have as many letters as CNN.

Robin Williams, it's not. But certainly more wry than Dan "Gore's got a mule in his pants but Dubya's drivin' the plow" Rather's folksy riffs on election night.

MSNBC has cheerfully sent the studly Williams out on the talk show circuit, where his good looks and quick wit help wave the flag.

CNN's decline and fall may well have occurred because it lost its young and hip edge, especially against the other cable news entities. Fox, loud, contentious and right wing, has come on strong. And MSNBC is giving even more indications that the cable net is aware of sex appeal and ratings.

I was watching MSNBC doing non-election updates the day after Thanksgiving. MSNBC, instead of presenting news on a proper news set, or even in a phony newsroom, had instead gone for a bus terminal look. People were walking and talking and strolling around. The only thing missing was a cappuccino cafe, a newsstand and a homeless guy asking for change.

But most male viewers' focus had to be on reporter Mika Brzezninski, who was perched perkily on a desk, behind which was an expert on something. They were talking about politics, I think, and may or may not have made a point or two in their discussion. I'm a little unclear because Mika was wearing a hiked-up skirt, her legs were crossed fetchingly and it was more than distracting. In fact, Mika has one terrific looking pair of legs.

Save your sexist rants. I'm sure if Brian Williams sat in a pair of yodel shorts and lederhosen, you ladies (and others) might have had a similar reaction. And if Mika is insulted at my saying she has a terrific pair of legs, I'm sorry, I'm a man and am required to think and act piggishly whenever possible. And, hey, it wasn't my idea to have you sit like that.

And yes, I'm sure it helped ratings more than the conversation about minor things like the fate of the country would.

That NBC crew may be the prettiest squad of newscasters in the biz. Campbell Brown, who is covering the White House under the Bush residency, looks like she just stepped out of a fashionable Republican Women's Club meeting. She has the straightest teeth in the world.

Before the big purge, CNN didn't bother making really good looks a priority. Okay, Willow Bay. Otherwise, they seemed stuck with the delusion that journalistic skills and knowledge of a topic count more than studliness.

It is safe to say a not-particularly-attractive newsie has to be twice as good to stay on the air as a hottie counterpart. To be honest, if Michelle Pfeiffer was asking a far-flung correspondent—or even near-flung correspondent—"How are things in Glocca Morra?" I'd be more likely to watch that than a similar newscast anchored by Roseanne. (Although, come to think of it, I'd pay cash money to see Roseanne go head-to-head with Chris Matthews.)

I suspect women would be more inclined to watch Brad Pitt do the news, than, say, Burl Ives, if only because Burl Ives is dead. I *think* Burl Ives is dead. Okay I'll pick somebody else. How about veteran character actor M. Emmet Walsh? You satisfied? I mean, this isn't science we're doing here; I don't expect to win a Pulitzer or anything. To be honest, this piece is pretty much just filler, a thumbsucker essay designed merely to entertain you with amusing anecdotes and get a lovely, very even smile from Campbell Brown if ever our paths should cross.

But let me make a serious point. When the celery's in the soup and the chicken's in the barn, (Whose barn? What barn? My barn.), TV is no different than newspapers. In the midst of disaster, you don't care what the reporter looks like, just whether he or she gets it right. When the big Northridge quake rumbled through L.A. in '94, the best guy on the story was Fox's gray fox, David Garcia, a former network type who brought a sense of *gravitas* to the issue. In other words, he knew his shit, and he looked like he knew his shit. And nobody laughed at him when he wore his adventurer's hat and his khaki photographer's vest or a journalist jacket you can order from Travelsmith along with blue blazers with 93 zippable pockets and emergency mosquito netting.

Because Garcia looked as if he'd earned the right to wear an outfit that would be laughable on some 26-year-old who thinks "trembler" is another term for earthquake. Garcia ran circles around the competition—figuratively, anyway.

Speaking of figures, aside from the network-morning-show fat weatherman, where are the porksters on the tube? About half the country's citizens could use a wideload sign slapped on his or her back, but where are their representatives on the news?

I guess what I'm saying—and with me it is usually just a guess—is if you aren't attractive, consider another career. Or don't, if you don't mind prejudice and a challenge. Neil Young, Mick Jagger and Cher never realized they couldn't sing until it was too late and they were already successful. As for you little people, pug-uglies and little old ladies? Leave your résumé with the secretary; we'll, ah, get back to you.

# The News Director's After-Sweeps Speech
## (A Transcript)

Testing. Testing. Is this live? *(Squeeeeeeeeeeeeeeek!!!! )* . . . Where's Miltie from audio? . . . When did he quit? . . . I fired him? Oh. *(Clears throat)*

Can you hear me in the back? You can't? Then how did you hear that? *(waits for non-existent laugh)* Tough room.

But seriously, folks, I want to thank all of you for coming to our little after-sweeps howgozit gathering. Good turnout for a voluntary meeting . . . and with all the, ah, numerous bomb threats we've been getting. Please enjoy the Kool-Aid and Cheez-Its.

As you know, these last sweeps have been a little disappointing. But let's not forget our one-half percent share improvement in 55-and-older adults. Sure, the boys in research call them "dearly beloved" viewers, but a gain is a gain.

I'm not placing the blame for our ratings shortfall on anyone specifically. Certainly I made some mistakes myself. For instance, I think some of the budget cuts I ordered were a little extreme. In retrospect, I now realize it was a bad idea to sell all the crew vans and live trucks.

In my own defense, there is an excellent public transportation system in our fine city. I just didn't anticipate how many of you would have trouble using it.

So, as you know, a lot of our news didn't make air until the following day, if then. We all recall that dark day when reporter Harrison Bleen and shooter Jake Scuzzu apparently took the

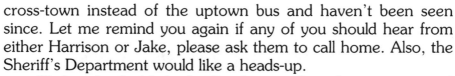

cross-town instead of the uptown bus and haven't been seen since. Let me remind you again if any of you should hear from either Harrison or Jake, please ask them to call home. Also, the Sheriff's Department would like a heads-up.

I'll also take the blame for the plan to sell snacks, ice cream and sodas out of our satellite truck. But you know, I wasn't the one who left the box of Creamsicles on top of the editing station overnight.

If I had it to do over, I probably wouldn't have written my infamous "no more days off until morale improves" memo. As your union rep informed me during the, ah, wildcat strike, that's a violation of section 5 sub paragraph (b) of your contract. So you have my apologies there. And no hard feelings. The tires on my Explorer were Firestones, so in a sense you were doing me a favor by slashing them.

To whoever let the stinkbomb loose on the set during our six o'clock news, we will find you. I'd like to thank the FCC for letting us off with a small fine after our anchor Max, instead of saying, "Yadda yadda, here's the news," ad libbed, "Holy mother of skunkfarts, who cut the cheese?"

Let's see, what else? Ah! Again, my bad for the three part series tied in to *Temptation Island*. A number of people have told me it was no less than a shameless promotion of a fluffy network primetime broadcast, and an embarrassment to our news department. That's a little harsh. We're all in the synergy business. But I probably should have checked to make sure *Temptation Island* was on *our* network before running it.

Now, on to some more positive matters. Big round of posthumous congratulations to the late Bob Haggasaw in engineering who worked so hard to get the software glitches out of the new automatic studio cameras. I can speak for each and every one of you when I say how greatly saddened we were by his tragic, uh, crushing to death. Wait . . . Is it *crushing* to death, or *being crushed* to death? Anyone? Tomato, tomahto, I guess.

You'll be happy to know that the damage to our news set was covered by insurance after all, and won't be deducted from your paycheck, as I threatened last week.

Okay, about our sweeps series. Again, I'll take the responsibility for changing the name of Jenny Hallwassel's series from "Breast Self-Exams: Detecting Cancer Before It's Too Late" to "Let's Grab Some Hooters."

I was just trying to reward all the hard work done by the boys in sales for getting all five parts sponsored by our good friends at, ah, *(mumbles)* Hooters.

Sports! You guys had some nine exclusive stories you broke during sweeps! Nine! No, fine, go ahead. Applaud. Nitpicking? Sure. But I do wish there was at least one of them we didn't have to retract. Nevertheless, I congratulate you on your enthusiasm, enterprise, and your . . . ah, spelling.

Just one, ah, suggestion regarding your exclusive report that the Farnwell High Fighting Ducks—careful on those Spoonerisms, fellas—had dropped out of the state championships because they were all gay. Make a phone call! That way you can prevent these kinds of errors . . . and lawsuits.

Okay, sure. I'm the guy who put pay phones in the newsroom. But I always have change and my door is always open . . . missing, actually. No sense crying over spilled milk, or in this case, the $350,000 in arson damage to the high school.

Next item. People, I've been in this business for more than a few years, I know how rumors get around, but please realize there are people involved. Anyway, spreading lies and rumors about me . . . saying I left my wife for a man . . . really hurts my feelings, and of course, those of Monsignor O'Donoghue. Then, as now . . . we're just good friends.

Now then, I shouldn't have to mention this again, but I will. Our newsroom flashcam is to be used only for actual news breaks, not for making pornographic videos. So, no more of that. Or at least get a director who knows the difference between patching to a VCR, and sending it out over the air.

We had what, Bob? Is Bob here? Yes, Bob Lipinki, our station counsel, everyone . . . What? Right, some 5,000 phone calls came in before the system crashed. That includes the 2,000 calls of complaint and the 3,000 or so asking for a date with Vicki

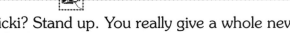

. . . Where are you, Vicki? Stand up. You really give a whole new meaning to the word "flashcam."

Okay, cutting to the chase here. A number of you have been kind enough to drop by the office and ask me about my own future . . .

Some have speculated I'm out . . . fired . . . *(interrupted by applause)*. Please, ah, if you could hold the cheering and applause until the end . . . Thank you. Others might have heard I'll be kept on as acting news director until my trial date.

I have good and bad news. The bad news is, starting next week, you will have a new news director to break in . . . Again, please hold the cheering until I'm finished, okay? The good news? I've landed a job as a news consultant.

Thank you and God bless . . . um, America.

# Sex and the Egomaniac

Heywood Broun, or perhaps it was Bono, once said, "Repartee is the art of what you wish you'd said."

People in TV news are required to think on their feet. They operate under a lot of pressure, and sometimes there aren't enough chairs. Field reporters, particularly, must stay ever-vigilant to make sure the anchor doesn't try to re-establish dominance at their expense by asking them a question they can't answer at the end of a live shot.

Producers and anchors sometimes go over the story in advance to figure an appropriate question for the anchor to ask, and reporter to answer. This makes everybody look smart and keeps the tape packages shorter for the all-important story flow the consultants want.

Some anchors just fire away, or intentionally make the reporter look stupid or unprepared:

- "Thank you for that, Larry. How many uncles overall did the victim have?
- "Ann, you mention police still think the killer is loose in the neighborhood. Just when exactly was that area incorporated, and how many square miles does it include?
- "Bob, you mentioned police are looking for the kidnap victim's stolen Buick now. How many horses is that baby packing under the hood?"

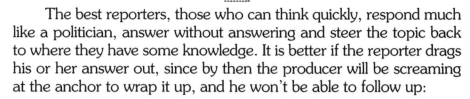

The best reporters, those who can think quickly, respond much like a politician, answer without answering and steer the topic back to where they have some knowledge. It is better if the reporter drags his or her answer out, since by then the producer will be screaming at the anchor to wrap it up, and he won't be able to follow up:

- "You ask about uncles, and that is a good question, but let me point out at this time none of the victim's uncles have even been brought up by police as potential suspects, which means police have an investigation on their hands. Where that will lead, only time will tell."
- "Thank you for asking that. I was talking with officials earlier and they said it isn't the square mileage that concerns them, or even as you suggest, the incorporation date. No, it goes much further, for this is a very clever criminal, according to my sources, and police, as I mentioned earlier, are warning residents . . ."
- "How many? Enough horses to get down the highway, that's for sure. As I mentioned earlier, police say the suspected kidnapper was seen driving away at a high rate of speed. And once again, let me run down the description of the car. It was . . ."

This ability to think quickly is not restricted just to on-air types trying to deflect a rogue question or salvage a live shot that went squirrelly when the package wasn't ready in time.

When they live in Hollywood, people in TV sometimes come in contact with real celebrities. Occasionally their ability to think on their feet is put to good use.

This is the best example I'd heard of during my stint in Candyland. I didn't eyewitness it, so I won't reveal the name of the big-time TV star, even thought I'm sure everyone coming to America in the next 48 hours would stand around trying to guess until asked to move on by some Beverly Hills cop.

A beautiful reporter told me of the time she was at the same party as the superstar. The man kept eyeing her, and eventually sent one of his entourage over to fetch her. Introductions were made, and the Superstar told the woman he was sure they had met before. He hadn't just seen her on television.

She smiled, flattered, and noted that she had once been at another party the superstar had attended, and they'd met then.

The Superstar smiled and said. "Refresh my memory, baby. Did I fuck you?"

The reporter's response earned her immediate entry into the Grace Under Fire Hall of Fame.

"Baby," she said, "If you'd fucked me, I *guarantee* you'd remember me."

# Bites 'r' Us:
# The Cure for Bad MOS

*In TV news, MOS is the "Man on the Street" who is interviewed for a story. (MOSs may also include women and kids.)*

Hey, Mr. News Director, how many times have you heard your assignment editor say this?

"Gee, sorry, boss. We missed that fire because Joe the Reporter was still doing his MOSs at the car crash, and just didn't make it there on time."

How often have you had a perfectly good story ruined by bad MOSs? People with bad accents. Those who waste your reporter's time by saying, "Sorry didn't see the shooting." People who don't want to go on the air because of possible retribution. Eyewitnesses who ramble.

Yes, getting that perfect MOS soundbite for your story *can* be difficult. But new phony research from our very own consultant service now proves beyond a doubt that MOSs are a critical part of your news. Why? Don't know. Needs more research. Lord, don't the money roll in.

Face it, Mr. News Director—you don't want *your* career depending on some schmuck on the street who doesn't know what to say, or how to say it. That's why we at Bites 'r' Us are offering you everything you need for *the* perfect MOSs, the first time, every time.

How do we do this? No, not by sending a crew out with yours. We get the perfect bite *before the story even happens!* Over the past three years, our camera crews have been scouring America, recording all kinds of people saying just the right thing in just the right way.

We've taped thousands of men and women of all races, creeds and colors giving the snappy soundbite that will make your news *come alive!!*

Order our *Basic Bites 'r' Us Package* now, and here's what you get:

We start with 5,000 MOS sound bites for any occasion, indexed by subject matter. Men, women and children saying, "It was amazing"; "He was a quiet boy"; "I can't believe it"; "I'm in shock!"; "I'm bummed out." And much, much more.

These bites have been shot with geographic- and weather-neutral backgrounds. All bites are five seconds or less, so your news never slows down for draggy opinions, stutterers, or vocalized pauses that can ruin the best MOS.

But, hey! We know even generic bites can grow stale, or get used up in this high-story-count world we live in. So our package also includes fresh bites, some 500 in all, delivered each month!

And that's just our Basic Package. With the *Deluxe Package,* in addition to everything listed above, you'll get Sports Bites 'r' Us and Weather Bites 'r' Us. Angry fans, snow-covered neighbors, they're all there, all ready at a moment's notice to be inserted into a sports story or weather package.

Got rain coming? You'll have bites ready like, "It's good for the sassafras"; "There goes my picnic!"; and "I'd better get some sandbags."

Did your local favorites fail to make the playoffs? You'll get devoted fans saying "Wait'll next year!"; "We need a new coach"; and "They really suck!"

And if you act now, you can save 25 percent off our regular price for our Bites 'r' Us *Sweeps Spectacular Package.* In addition to everything listed above, you'll get special MOS soundbites designed to fit your specific sweeps package.

Doing a series on local strip clubs? We'll send you a Bites 'r' Us package of outraged opponents saying "Not in my back yard";

"It's not fair to the kids"; and "There go my property values!" Also, proponents saying "It's a free country"; "Hey, it's the 21st century"; and "Nudity is protected by the Constitution."

Not convinced yet? We'll send you a free demo package that you can use FREE on your air for thirty days! (Sorry, not valid during sweeps.) If your news costs don't drop and ratings rise, just send it back, and there's no charge to you.

But if you agree these are the best darn MOS sound bites you've ever heard, just sign up for a year and that first month is still free!

Listen to these endorsements.

> Thanks, Bites 'r' Us. Because of you, I've been able to lay off two crews and three reporters. Talk about a money saver!
>
> —ND in top 100 market

> This is great! Your MOSs are better than any we've done, and cheaper!
>
> —ND in top 50 market

> Hey, we don't use them, but by buying them with your market-exclusive guarantee, we keep the competition from using them!
>
> —ND in top 25 market

So act soon. Before the competition does!

# God Love the Assignment Desk, the Bastards

The assignment desk is the hub of any newsroom. An assignment manager (also know as an "assignment editor" and by more colorful names) who is worth his or her salt must be a nimble magician. Several are shot and killed by disgruntled reporters and cameramen each year.

To stay alive and succeed at a near impossible task, an assignment manager must do the following simultaneously:

- Take in and evaluate vast amounts of information from press releases, city news services, police and fire scanners, the morning newspaper, the tabloids, the network feeds, and broadcasts of other local stations.
- Know the location of all his reporters, shooters and live trucks, including favorite in-station hiding places and secret saloons. He must know how to get them to any point where news is happening and deliver the information accurately over a two-way. He must schedule interviews, satellite time and one week a year to recover from his nervous breakdown.
- Keep track of hours worked and avoid union penalties for overtime and late lunches of reporters and crews where such quaint rules still apply. He must know both the union meal time and the actual meal time to know if a cameraman is actually eating, which he does on company time, or running his personal business, which he does during union meal times. Or vice versa.

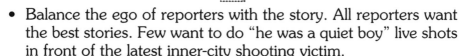

- Balance the ego of reporters with the story. All reporters want the best stories. Few want to do "he was a quiet boy" live shots in front of the latest inner-city shooting victim.
- Instantly divert crews and reporters to more important or time-critical stories, while mollifying the reporter who'd been setting up his enterprise piece for months and now must cover a fire that will be out by the time he gets there.
- Coordinate and talk to the station chopper jock, help coordinate his live hits, direct him, and try not to make him fly past bingo fuel points and turn his chopper into a plow.
- Help coordinate live shots (no matter how meaningless), live teases, live-on-tape teases, tape feeds, equipment troubles, and getting a second man to a live shot when a cable run must go through a carwash and up a ten-story building.
- Refrain from giggling like a schoolgirl every time a manager runs the latest consultant-driven non-story past him, telling him it's a hot story that must get done.
- Talk good reporters into bad stories and bad reporters into good stories.
- Be thick-skinned enough to handle constant complaints shouted at him from above and below.
- Refrain from getting too high when everything falls into place, or too low when it all goes to hell in a hurry. Then he must come back and do the same thing the next day for ridiculously low pay and even more ridiculously low respect.
- Be invisible. Assignment editors, much like umpires and refs, are doing their job if they aren't drawing attention to themselves.
- Be schizophrenic and the owner of multiple simultaneous personalities. He must be a sweet-talker without reason, a whip-cracker without authority, a suck-up both to management and to story sources.
- Originate news when no news exists, control time when too much news breaks at once. He must take the blame for flames that go out, victims who walk away from fatal crashes; for locations that have suddenly disappeared, crews that are late, reporters who are lazy and equipment that breaks down. And the times he screws up.

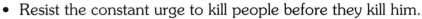

- Resist the constant urge to kill people before they kill him.
- Keep an eye out to know when it is time to leave his addictive but non–career-enhancing job and move on before he gets an obit that reads, "Heart attack at age 31," or "Cause of death: two behind the ear."

# The First of Two Good Assignment Editor Stories

Before the age of microwave relays, a hard-charging reporter named Jim Clark (see story on page 109) was coming in from the field with a story he insisted must make air for the six o'clock news. Jim Clark insisted all his stories must make air.

The station had recently leased a helicopter. However, it did not yet have a landing pad at the station, and as the station was located in a populated area, the chopper could not land close to the station, either.

Even so, the reporter insisted that the helicopter meet him at National Airport, where he would climb aboard with his tape, and fly to the station.

"And then what?" the assignment editor asked, incredulously.

"You go down into the basement and grab the Red Cross emergency equipment kit. Get out the blanket. Then grab an intern and go up on the roof. Open the blanket and I'll drop the tape in the blanket."

The assignment manager knew better than to argue with a reporter whose nickname was "Madman," and did as he was told.

He and the intern were soon on the roof of the station holding the blanket open as the chopper came thumping over the horizon. It was low, and started to slide into a hover over the blanket. The duo on the roof could see Clark leaning out of the helicopter, tape in hand.

We now pause quickly for a quick lesson in aviation and physics.

Lesson One: A fixed-wing aircraft is kept aloft by air passing under its wings and providing lift.

Lesson Two: A helicopter is not.

How does a helicopter remain airborne? That's right, kids: by deflecting massive amounts of air downward under its main rotor, a miniature wing that provides lift.

And what was under the rotor on that rooftop as it moved into its hover? That's right: two guys holding a blanket wide open. And what did the blanket do when the helicopter drifted over them? Right again. It acted like a spinnaker hit by a hurricane. The downdraft sent the intern and the assignment manager flying and nearly blew them off the roof before they let go of the blanket, which blew into a nearby tree.

Undaunted, Madman insisted on a second try—this time without the blanket—and successfully tossed the tape down, where it made air.

# Second Good Assignment Editor Story

My dog had died. For reasons known only to me and my shrink I told the assignment manager about it. I don't want to embarrass him so I'll give you only his initials, which are Jack Noyes.

A few days after the death of my dog, Jack called me over to the assignment desk. A reporter was about to do a live shot. She'd been at the same locale several nights running and had been visited each night by a collarless, ownerless, filthy but friendly dog. The manager insisted I take the dog home.

"That's the dumbest idea I've ever heard," I said gently, hoping to spare his feelings. I'd forgotten that after a few years of getting their teeth kicked in every night, assignment managers don't have feelings.

"Listen. The dog was abandoned. We got no more story there. We leave it, it goes to the pound and gets the big lethal."

"My kids aren't ready for another dog, yet," I said. "Certainly not some mutt off the street."

"But it's a great dog. Tell you what—"

"No!" I explained.

"Just hear me out. I'll have our reporter bring it in. You don't like it? You don't have to take it home."

"No."

Naturally, Jack took that to meant he should bring the dog in. The dog appeared friendly enough and attracted the attention of everyone in the newsroom. It wagged its filthy tail, licked every hand it could get at and bit no one. Everyone was under the impression—probably because the assignment manager told them—that I was taking the dog home for good.

"No, absolutely not," I said to a chorus of boos.

"All right," the assignment manager said. "I apologize for telling everyone it's your dog. What I really meant is you're taking it home on a trial basis. If you don't like it, I'll take it back. Honest. I promise."

I took the dog home. When I got there, my oldest son, John was happy to meet the dog, while Andrew burst into tears. The next morning, Andrew started to play with the dog. John, with more sense then his old man, said "Dad, it's really too soon to get another dog. And you better get rid of it before it's too late"

I called the assignment manager right away and told him I was bringing the dog back.

"What dog? Who is this?" Jack answered.

"You know damn well what dog."

"I don't know anything about a dog."

"Yes, you do."

"Why are you bringing this dog of yours to the station?"

"It didn't work out."

"What has that got to do with me? It's your dog."

"Oh no. You promised to take him back if . . ."

"I did no such thing. I'm calling security!"

Jack refused to take the animal back. The dog eventually was owned by Faith Ford of *Murphy Brown* and *Norm* fame, but that's another story.

But it proved two things:

1. Some dogs have all the luck.
2. Never believe an assignment manager. They lie like a dog.

# Food You Can't Eat at News You Can Use

One of the nicer aspects of entertainment reporting is free grub. Interviews, movie junkets and major awards ceremonies usually involve vittles for the media gang covering the event.

Sometimes, it is quite decent. Over the years, the best event has been the Golden Globes, where food is served on real china and with tableclothed splendor. (The Golden Globes is run by the foreign entertainment press, who know what media want.) In contrast, many other events offer sandwiches rolled up in plastic wrap and some *crudités* to go along with the crudities.

Why the free food? Partly, it's to suck up to the media. Partly, it's because producers want to put free food out for the celebrity participants, and if there is a media guy within 100 yards of free food, he'll find it and eat it anyway. Partly, it's because these events can easily drag on for four to five hours or more, and a man or woman has gotta eat.

Not all producers understood that. For years, one big-time producer was considered among the cheapest when it came to media food. I remember one awards event where the only thing he served was coffee. Soon after, an *Entertainment Tonight* photographer, noting the lack of food at an event, ordered pizzas for everyone and sent the bill to the producer. The producer stormed up to the cameraman, who explained in the nicest terms what the situation was, and persuaded the producer to pay the tab. After that, all his events were catered.

# You've Been Bumped, Hotshot

Few things cut to the quick for a reporter more than getting bumped, or spiked. Much of my act was fluff, so I was sometimes deemed a purveyor of the irrelevant, and because I could be a general pain in the ass many show producers took glee in canceling my act.

Being bumped meant you'd wasted your day, your talent, your life, your career, your time on earth. Not to mention the time spent slaving over your story and bullshitting with the editor who cut it. Even if the piece could be salvaged for another newscast or another day, your ego had been given a lubricant-free proctoscopy. Being bumped, in a word, sucked.

Some memorable examples:

I was live from the premiere of the first movie of the holiday season in L.A. Pretty good story in a company town. Five minutes before my spot, which was kicking the show, the station's chopper was hovering over a discarded grocery bag in some reeds. Trouble was, the citizen who'd called it in to the police had said something about just maybe there was a dead baby in the bag. Dead baby bumps Big Guy.

Was it just my ego that caused my upset? Not this time. There was a pretty good chance the bag would not be plucked until after the end of the newscast. That turned out to be so. But say the bag *had* been recovered. The contents inside were either a dead baby, or groceries, or a bag of trash. If it was a baby, the audience would be exposed to that horror at mealtime. What purpose is served by showing the corpse of an infant removed from a paper bag?

Had it been an empty bag, or trash, or even groceries, a top story in a company town would have been bumped to watch a police helicopter practice litter removal. Incidentally, it was filled with trash.

I had a live interview ready to go for an after-Academy Award live show. It was bumped so Mr. Blackwell could offer his description of the attendees' outfits.

I've been bumped more than once by producers who can't backtime (make the newscast end on schedule). Although, in one spectacular incident of time shifting, I was once assigned a fifteen-minute chitchat with two anchors after the producer mistimed the end of a one-hour newscast by a quarter of an hour.

One time, I was bumped and didn't mind a bit, even though I was kept off the air by a police chase.

Through a series of misunderstandings, an executive show producer had decided to tease an exclusive interview I would conduct with Edgar Bronfman, Jr., new chairman/owner of Universal Studios, who hadn't talked to anyone in the media since the buyout. The interview had been teased not only on our air but also on commercials on radio stations.

One problem: the producer hadn't talked to me about it. When I got to work, I found out that what he had set up was getting a camera into an old Jewish home where Edgar Bronfman *Senior*, the all-but-retired father of the power behind Universal, was visiting to donate some money.

I screamed and yelled, especially when they sent a crew and all they got was the presentation and a fleeing Bronfman saying "I'm not answering questions about Universal or the sale."

Swell. I was convinced/ordered/threatened and ended up taking one for the team. I wrote a carefully worded piece of crapola, that essentially had nothing to do with what was teased, but of course had my face attached to it.

My hit time was 9:45 P.M. At 9:30, some bozo on a motorcycle started leading police around the area. The producer (who was also embarrassed) and I hit our knees and prayed the chase would continue for at least a half hour. It did, and the station covered every minute of it. The piece never ran, and I got credit for taking one for the team.

That was one chase I didn't mind. Calls of complaint? None.

# Do Not Go Gently . . .
# See a Surgeon

In television news, being wizened and wise ain't what it once was. In fact, age is a barrier to progress. Ageism runs rampant. It's not necessarily just out of dislike for geezers, but mostly because young people work cheaper and stay healthier, saving bottom-line money all around. And, as any good Marine knows, it's easier to train someone from scratch than retrain him from bad habits. (I was in the Air Force, where they trained you to stay away from drunken Marines at the O Club.)

The Marine method works best for TV journalists. Instead of having to strip off all those layers of journalism from an experienced newsie, it's easier for management to break in a newcomer happy just to make a fifty-market jump.

Still, some people in the biz have managed to age gracefully—occasionally with the help of makeup breakthroughs and plastic surgery. Some, like me, even manage to last to the north side of the big five-oh before they finally get out.

There are, of course, some techniques for postponing the inevitable. Sucking up to management is one. Taking a cut in pay. Perhaps digitally rejiggering a photograph to put the GM in the arms of a whore.

When I was in my late forties, I decided to hide my aging process by dying my hair. There are products you can use at home that will dye your hair darker. They are also excellent for spot-staining the rug as well as any towels, walls or pets within a ten-foot radius.

Another problem with some of these products was that they left purple highlights. I looked like the bastard child of Phil Donohue and Cyndi Lauper.

For those of you about to hit a significant birthday, here are some suggestions on how to get through it:

1. Tell yourself you're only as young as you feel, unless you feel like crap. Then sit down and shut up.
2. Try to carve out some time to watch the intro of *60 Minutes*, and sit there going, "Younger than him . . . Her, too . . . Gawd, I though he was *dead! . . . Much* younger than him . . ." They never show Andy at the top of the show, but don't worry—everyone's younger than Andy.
3. Do not drink too much alcohol to celebrate the day. Anything less than a lethal dose is fine.
4. Have sex. Preferably with a partner.
5. Prepare yourself for increased short-term memory loss.
6. Don't exercise. Exercise is overrated. Three out of four doctors don't know squat. Coffee will or will not kill you. Let the good and bad cholesterol settle their differences amicably. Go where you wanna go, do what you wanna do, just remember to bring liniment, hot towels and an unguent.
7. Figure how much money you have left, and compare to how many years you expect to work and how long you expect to live after that. If they don't match, spend money faster to motivate yourself to earn more money.
8. Write Nielsen a nasty letter saying you wouldn't be part of one of their stinking surveys if they asked you to.
9. Prepare yourself for increased short-term memory loss
10. Count your blessings on the fingers of your hands. If you have to remove your shoes and socks, consider yourself lucky.

# Attila and the
# Bunny Do Lunch

Here's how it goes in the TV employment dodge: Nobody loves you unless they are reasonably certain somebody else loves you. Or they can get you cheaper before somebody else expresses their love for you.

You are never more valuable to a station than when they think someone else wants you. To show how this works, let me take you through a real-life adventure I went through.

It is six months before my contract is up. To deal from strength in the upcoming negotiations, it is wise to have a backup plan. My agent has found someone who is interested in acquiring me. Unfortunately, the news director in question has a nickname—Attila the Hun. This is not a good nickname for a news director you work for.

Nevertheless, I will lunch with Attila this noon. My agent said it could give us leverage. What could it hurt?

We will play a little game this lunch. Do a little fandango. My agent has told me Attila really wants another critic for the job, but since my agent knows the other critic is unavailable, she stirred up Attila's interest in me. I'm not interested in Attila, unless my station proves uninterested in me, in which case Attila is more appealing. Attila and I are like two betrayed lovers trying to get on with our lives and work up an interest in each other.

Right off the bat, Attila seems like a decent guy. But then, so does Hannibal Lecter when he keeps his mouth shut. Attila is full of flattery for me, always an endearing trait. He says he used to tell his feature reporters he wanted them to do their pieces just like I did. He says, if I come over he will feature me doing humorous, creative pieces, just like the good old days.

When the waiter brings Attila his rabbit stew, he spends a lot of time chewing, even more time removing little bones from his mouth, while I try not to stare.

"Damn, if I'd known there were so many little bones, I wouldn't have ordered it," Attila says.

"Well, don't choke," I respond, "I don't know the Heimlich maneuver."

"If I did choke to death at lunch with you, you'd be a hero in my newsroom," Attila says. There's a little wistfulness but also a sliver of pride in his voice. Attila, I realize, gets off on being hated. May even be why he ordered bunny for lunch—to see if I flinch. I don't. I don't have many dietary restrictions. Okay, one. After seeing *Babe*, that wonderful film about an adorable talking pig, I swore that for the rest of my life, despite my lifelong love of pork, that no matter the circumstance, I would never, but never *ever* eat a talking pig.

Over the years, I've learned a major key to success at the employment seduction game. Just as in love, the most successful players exude confidence and desirability.

This quality becomes most irresistible when the object of desire is already in the arms of another. When one has a relatively secure job, or is the object of courtship from several sources, that confidence and security give off the employment equivalent of a musk. If you're really good at it, your potential employer wants to rip off your duds and have you right on the lunch table— metaphorically.

Lunch isn't about lunch; it's about business, of course. Occasionally, though, the challenges of the mechanics of lunch itself can intrude. During an interview for a slot on a network show a few years back, my suitor spilled so much salad on himself I wondered if it was some sort of test. As croutons and wafer-thin slices of cucumber joined the argyle patterns of his sweater, as shreds of Romaine and slices of tomato garnished his lapel, I pondered my quandary—to splatter or not to splatter?

Does one ignore it, join in, or play along? Do you say, "I've always wanted to work on your show and, by the way, that endive goes well with your tie"? Or, "Bring me aboard and we'll fit together like a herringbone jacket and Thousand Island dressing"?

By the end of that meal, my potential employer had spilled so much food you could order from his ensemble, I was still spotless, and no job offer was forthcoming. Next time someone dribbles, I'm pouring my soup in my lap.

As for Attila, he got through the meal without choking, and told me to have my agent call him. In the world of contract negotiations, that's known as "serious interest." Of course my agent, being smart, first called the people I already worked for and told them there was "serious interest" in me from elsewhere. My agent is honest, always has been. Management, knowing she is honest, knows she is telling the truth, and there is indeed "serious interest" in me.

Now my employers have three choices:

Say bye-bye, and let the other party have me.

Make an immediate offer to renew me, thus avoiding a bidding war.

Wait to see if a bidding war ensues, or the interest wanes.

But because they believe there is serious interest in me elsewhere, that confirms I have value. No one trusts his own judgment fully, and this apparently provided the second opinion in my case that led to an immediate offer. We signed it, and shortly thereafter Br'er Rabbit's buddy Attila was fired. Not over letting me get away, not for being Attila, but for the tired old standby—failing to improve ratings.

# Discount Johnny, the Prince of Low Prices

For three months between TV news gigs, I worked as a host on a Financial News Network spin-off called "Telshoppe." The fact that neither Telshoppe nor FNN exists anymore should give you an indication of the positive impact I had on the operation. Telshoppe was created during the brief period in the mid-eighties when everyone and his sister wanted to sell stuff on TV.

With the increased penetration of cable, there were opportunities for organizations such as FNN to try to profit by selling gewgaws on the tube.

Credit where it's due: Telshoppe was a little different from most such shopping networks. We were loosey-goosey. We had six hosts selected from the fringes of news and entertainment, mostly for personality. No formal presentations for us. No hard sell on Telshoppe. Hell, there was no formal training. Just an audition and encouragement to show the product and read the phone number. It was a gas.

When the show first started, all we'd have to sell with was the product itself, an index card with basic info and prices, and a pat on the ass. Eventually, the show added little giveaway games and calls from viewers. The cast included an L.A. sportscaster who later ended up on KABC, Todd Donohoe, and a female TV personality and travel reporter who became the first female announcer on a game show, Michelle Roth. We all had fun— sometimes more fun than a profitable operation would want.

I was particularly loosey-goosey because I'd already landed my next job, as a lifestyle reporter in Boston. I had little to lose. I'd dubbed myself "Discount Johnny, the Duke of Deals, the Prince of Low Prices, the Meshuggeneh Maharajah of Markdown."

One night, while selling a trip to the Virgin Islands, I suggested that among the fun activities there would be "snorkeling, scuba diving and scouring the island for virgins."

That earned me a call into the office of the producer the next day. He informed me there had been some calls complaining about my remarks. I took the criticism with my usual evenhandedness.

"Screw those assholes. It's just a bunch of bluehairs out in Missouri. What do they know?"

"One of the callers was the chairman of the board," the producer said.

"Of what?" I responded.

"Of our company."

"Oh," I retorted.

The next night I suggested that among the fun activities down in the Virgin Islands were "scuba diving, snorkeling and *not* scouring the island for virgins." I guess the boss wasn't watching, because I wasn't fired.

One female host was given the honor of being the very first seller on the very first day the show began. She was handed a diamond bracelet, an index card with the words "diamond bracelet" on it and turned loose for a fifteen-minute session.

Somehow, she muddled through, getting more and more frustrated, but forcing a smile and selling her fool ass off. The instant the red light went out, the rest of us burst into spontaneous applause. She acknowledged it, her saleslady smile disappeared, and she shouted: "I quit my father's jewelry store to do this fucking shit?!"

Later on, Telshoppe doubled up its salespeople, figuring if we ran out of things to say about the product, at least we could talk to one another. One time, Michelle and I were selling a jewelry holder. It stood maybe a foot tall and looked like it came out of a Cracker Jack box. But, for once, we had some detailed promo copy to sell from, and we noted that the device contained "swing-out doors complete with stained glass windows."

That's what the copy said. In reality, it was made out of mashed tree leavings and Elmer's glue, assembled in the People's Democratic Republic of Kathielee, and peddled to people wanting to spruce up the Doublewide. My partner and I were demonstrating the features and swung out the tiny little doors. Just as Michelle began to extol the virtue of the cathedral glass, the tiny little piece of colored plastic started to slip loose and slide out of the cabinet entirely.

With lightning-like reflexes, Michelle pinned the plastic to the door with her fingernail. The day was saved. We really should have made it through. But we made eye contact and became two little kids who'd heard a fart in church. Instant giggles. The camera stayed tight on the product, while Michelle and I laughed as silently as possible, until there were tears rolling down our cheeks and words choking in our throats. Never had show business seemed a sillier occupation for adults.

We'd still be there if I hadn't raced out in a panic, believing (rightly) that Michelle would be professional enough to recover once the accelerant was removed from the fire.

Not that I needed a partner to give me the giggles. Telshoppe sold everything from porcelain Elvises, exercise gear that sometimes blew apart on camera, pasteboard cuckoo clocks and all manner of junk.

There were some quality items, however, and one proved my undoing. We had all sold relatively inexpensive automatic cameras often on the show. To make them more enticing, they came with a camera bag filled with goodies—extra film, filters, lens tissue, batteries, a book on how to take great pictures, and so forth. The whole package ran about a hundred bucks, if I remember.

Early one Sunday morning, I was informed I had a much more expensive camera to sell. I don't remember the brand, but it was priced out the door at something over five hundred dollars. I could tell by looking at the camera body that it was a professional quality model. But there was a glitch. There was no lens attached.

Professional cameras feature interchangeable lenses. A professional photographer might have several camera bodies hanging around his neck and a variety of lenses to mix and match.

I figured that because only the camera body was in front of me, this was what we were selling. I checked with a floor manager before I went on whether that was the case. He checked upstairs. Nobody knew. They promised to get back to me.

"Meanwhile, what should I say?" I asked.

"Tell them you don't know," I was told.

Fair enough. That's why I was getting the big bucks. Amazingly, inspiration hit and I thought of a foolproof selling technique. I'd admit my ignorance and let the viewer provide the intelligence. The potential buyer would likely be a serious photographer who would know if the price was right for the body alone or if a lens should be included. Cork, you're a freakin' genius, boy.

"We sell a lot of inexpensive cameras here on Telshoppe," I began confidently. "Good cameras for the everyday user. Today is different. Today we are selling this amazing camera, a professional-quality camera for only $549. I am certain a professional photographer will know if that is a great price for this camera with or without a lens. Because, quite frankly, I don't know. Nobody seems to know here at Telshoppe, if the lens is included, and if it is, what kind or size lens it is.

"But you, as a professional photographer, *would* know," I said in my unctuously flattering voice. Then, remembering techniques used to fill time while peddling the less expensive cameras, I reached for the previously unexamined camera bag that came with the camera body and/or lens.

"I can't tell you if you get a lens with this camera, but I *can* tell you what you *do* get." Watch me, Willy Loman, and learn a couple of sales techniques from the master, I thought.

I opened the bag and looked in.

"You get, um, first of all, this lovely case the uh, camera comes in. And, of course,"— I reached into the bag—"this lovely strap for the lovely bag for your camera. And . . ." I looked into the bag, and pulled out the last item.

". . . and of course you get this free package of lens tissue for the lens you may or may not get . . ."

And those were the last words out of my mouth. How absurd was this? Two months earlier I'd been a top Hollywood film critic working for the number one television station in Los Angeles. Now I was standing in a cold, near-empty studio on a Sunday morning, peddling stuff I knew next to nothing about, including a six hundred dollar camera that came with a buck and a half's worth of lens tissue for a lens that may or may not come with it.

I could not speak, I could not breathe. I began to laugh until tears ran down my cheeks. Before they hit the floor, the station had dipped to a break and someone escorted me off, as another host got ready to take over.

I recovered in a few minutes. The lensless camera was withdrawn until someone could figure out if the lens came with it. (To this day, I don't know.)

The boss called me into the office the next day. I jumped the gun.

"Hey if you're gonna chew me out for yesterday, don't bother. How the hell am I gonna sell one of those stupid cameras if I don't know if a lens comes with it?"

"I called you in to congratulate you."

"For what?"

"For selling a half dozen cameras."

Discount Johnny, the Duke of Deals, might have been a legend if his career had not been stopped tragically short.

# You Can't Quit Me.
# I'm Fired!

I'm an aviation buff and believe that pound for pound, word for word, aviation has the best little sayings of all. Many are safety oriented, such as, "A midair collision can spoil your whole day," and "When landing an airplane, there's nothing more worthless than runway behind you and altitude above you."

Here is one that, with a few words changed, is appropriate for TV news—and many other high-risk professions. It goes, "There are only two kinds of retractable-gear pilots: those who have landed with their gear up, and those who someday will."

Translated into TV, it goes, "There are only two kinds of TV employees: those who have been fired, and those who someday will be."

Actually, that's not true. There are *three* kinds of TV employees: those who have been fired, those who someday will be, and those who have been fired and will be again.

If you have kind of a Marquis de Sade thing going, you've come to the right profession. When it comes to the act of getting fired, it's like being guillotined with a butter knife—inefficient and painful. The firing of TV talent ranks right up there with being let go by the mob, except the mob sends flowers.

(At the beginning of 2001, it was a bloodbath out there. CNN was in the process of carefully pruning the deadwood from its staff with the grace and elegance of Sasquatch trying on lingerie.)

For those of you starting out in the bidness, or considering a career in television, exiting a position should be of some interest to you, particularly if you're a sensitive soul.

Based on anecdotal evidence, personal experience and my voracious reading habits, here is a pretty good detailing of how you might expect it to go when you're—how can I put this without appearing insensitive?—shit-canned.

So read it and weep. Also, please remember this is only a sample; your experience may vary. Not valid in Vermont, Idaho, or Puerto Rico. Applicable taxes apply. Void where prohibited. Caution: in some states voiding where prohibited may be a fireable offense, so check with Human Resources first, as if *they* have a clue.

# The Firing

First, the Turk* taps you on your shoulder and says, "Coach wants to see you. Bring your playbook."

You trot upstairs, where some grim-looking drew-the-short-straw exec says, "We've decided to go in a different direction." Literally translated, that means management has royally screwed up, we're losing money, gotta cut warm bodies. We stay. You go. Don't let the door hit you on the ass.

An associate is always present to document any death threats or calls for help, or to take a bullet for the boss in case the ex-employee goes postal.

You are given a document to sign by which you promise, in exchange for moneys due you anyway, to go quietly, not make a fuss, not rip management in the media, not shoot up the newsroom, nor drop a virus into the office computer.

---

*An acquaintence who read a draft of this asked me why, in an otherwise ethnically neutral article, I chose to offend Turks. I explained to him, as I explain to you now, that it's a term pro football uses. For reasons unknown, the guy the coach sends to fetch a player about to be cut from the team is always referred to as "the Turk." And he alway says the same thing to the player: "Coach wants to see you. Bring your playbook." The player must turn in his playbook so he doesn't sell it to the highest bidder. In TV, the Turk may be the boss' secretary, or some kind of boss toady, or just some passing stranger who's wandered into the newsroom.

When you return to your office, there is a fresh box of complimentary Kleenex on your desk and a large person in uniform standing by it. He is either armed or carrying a large flashlight with extra batteries, and not afraid to use it. He is there to protect the newsroom, watch you pack, confiscate any dirty magazines you don't want to take home and walk you to the door, at the point of a gun if necessary.

Your computer no longer works because you are no longer a person there.

Your phone no longer works because you are no longer a person there.

If you're Talent, you will not get to say farewell to your audience, because you are no longer a person there.

Keep in mind that these people who have deemed you an unperson were the same people slapping you on the back at the Christmas party, and asking you to take one for the team and skip your daughter's First Communion to work. They were the same smiling folk who gave you a handshake for all those years of faithful service, for the overtime hours worked without compensation, for the soccer games missed, for the overall devotion to your job above and beyond the call of duty. You have a spotless record, no history of violence; you are a total professional. But they treat you like a criminal because it's more convenient to do so and because you are no longer a person there.

Now that you are no longer a person there, they lock themselves away in their management offices and write their memos that ask why, for heaven's sake, is morale so low?

To help you from getting caught by surprise, here are some of the warning signs your stay will not be a long one:

1. Your desk has been moved outdoors.
2. Your sweeps series has been slotted at 30 seconds tops, including lede, tag, tax and tip.
3. The boss suggests you test the new electric powerline warning system on the microwave truck because he "doesn't want to risk someone important."
4. Your station has been bought by Aryan Communications Corp., and you're Jewish.

5. Your face in the current promos has been digitally deleted.
6. Your car is towed each day from your reserved parking spot.
7. You are assigned to a bureau that just closed.
8. You find a skinned rabbit in your back yard. (This is also a sign you may be cheating on your wife with a psycho.)
9. You mention John F. Kennedy, and everyone thinks you mean the guy who died in the plane crash.
10. You're reassigned from anchoring the six to introducing the "Star Spangled Banner" sign-off tape.

# Hello, I Must Be Going . . .

My television career began in August 1977, the day after Elvis Presley died (according to the FBI, the events were unrelated) and ended in July 1997, the year the new owners at my station decided that they had low ratings with me, and they could have just as low ratings without me.

Not unexpectedly, I was given no opportunity to bid my fans a farewell on the air. (Fortunately, I was able to phone both of them individually.) Management is so untrusting of its employees, it gives them no last chance to have an emotional catharsis on the air, for fear the firee may take the opportunity to rip the bozos that run the dump.

Any book about the realities of television should deal with the end of the line, when it's all over and life must return to normal. I feel the denial of a final goodbye is a most cruel policy that should be changed. If only to provide that much overused and banal sense of "closure," a word that should be outlawed.

While it's too late for me, I've come up with the perfect solution. I've written an all-purpose, generic "Departure Speech," to be hereinafter and forthwith incorporated into all future agreements between Talent and Management.

## Cork's All-Purpose TV Goodbye Speech

I'd like to take a moment to announce (my resignation/my firing/my forcible removal) from (insert your television station or network here).

This is my (last/first and last) broadcast from this (anchor desk/sports desk/snake pit) and I leave with (mixed feelings/a heavy heart/a .357 Magnum tucked in my pants).

Before I go, however, I'd like to thank (you, the viewers/my attorneys/my favorite intern, Chlamydia). You have made my (stay at this station/years of service/recent trial) something I will (treasure/remember/seek therapy for) (for the rest of my days/until my non-compete runs out/for 25 to life).

Why am I (leaving/quitting/being run out of town on a rail)? Mostly it's because of (creative differences/management pinheads/the Mann Act).

I won't go into details of my (termination/resignation/castration) because (it is a private matter/the Federal Gag Order is still in effect/my "medication" makes me forget). However, I am (very happy/very unhappy/drunk as a skunk) after my decision to (resign/not fight the restraining order/head for the hills).

I treasure your (friendship/support/unsecured loans) and while I cannot (thank/write/boff) all of you, I hope to see you again (in the near future/at McDonald's/at my parole hearing).

In closing, I'd like to leave you with (this final thought/my sincerest thanks/the clap). Whenever you think of me, remember these words: ("God Bless You"/"Thanks for everything"/ "Bite me").

# Didn't You Used to Be . . . ?

I had been out of television for a couple of years. Some junket friends were in town, and I joined them for a movie and visit to the El Capitan theater, where Disney was having a *soiree* for *Toy Story II*.

After the screening, the building next to the theater was turned over to celebrants, celebs, schmoozers, hangers-on, players, punters, goniffs, actress/model/whatevers, friends of friends, people in cartoon character suits, studio suits, PR suits, agents, various children, and media and friends of media. The noshes were good, the company excellent, and there were balloons for the kids. Disney may be cheap, but they spend money smart.

I was walking back from the restroom when I was stopped by a loud "Hey!" and a tap on the shoulder.

I spun around and was facing a Hollywood producer. I knew he was a Hollywood producer because he was dressed like a Hollywood producer—black on black, with cologne that made him smell like a wet goat—and because he immediately told me he was a Hollywood producer. He was beaming from ear to ear, shook my hand vigorously and told me how much he liked my work. Liked it, hell, he *loved* it.

I was shocked and partially agog that two years after my demise I would be remembered with such enthusiasm. Sure, people still recognize me now and then, and many a time I've spotted that curious, blank, geez-I-know-him-from-somewhere expression. But this particular look was free of irony or doubt.

I'd seen that look before aimed at others. Usually it's a fan facing a celebrity. It's just a little short of adoration and, to be honest, it's very flattering and a little bit embarrassing to the recipient.

"So," he asked, "what are you up to?"

"Well, you know, a lot of projects in the fire. Movies I'm working on. A book. You know, the usual." That's Hollywood-speak for "not much," but he didn't pick up on it.

"Terrific. Did I say how much admire your work?"

"Again, my thanks."

He detected I didn't have a clue who he was.

"You remember my dad, of course."

"Of course. Who doesn't remember your dad?" I had no clue who his dad was, either.

"So anyway, I'm a producer, and I sure would welcome having the privilege of working with you someday."

No dummy I, I knew this might be a producer who would run with one of my movie projects.

"Say, do you have a card?" I asked.

The man's face lit up and he began slapping parts of his body as if he was being attacked by killer bees. Not a card to be found. He appeared crushed. But out came his wallet and a pen.

"Here, let me write down my number."

"Okay, thanks," I said, taking his phone number, which was written across his auto insurance guarantee card.

"I'll give you a shout," I said.

"May I say once again, what an honor it is seeing you again."

"You may, but the pleasure's mine."

We separated across a crowded room, and I couldn't wait to tell my friends.

"Just who did he think you were, anyway?"

You can always depend on friends for a cold slap of reality when you're feeling self-important.

Then it dawned on me. The Hollywood producer didn't think I was John Corcoran, former movie critic; he thought I was George Lucas, Hollywood player.

I bear, well, used to bear, a passing resemblance to Mr. *Star Wars*, especially around the beard and the double chin. Lucas is quite a few pounds lighter than me and several inches shorter, unless he's sitting on his wallet. During interviews, we had both remarked upon the facial resemblance. A half dozen times or so people have asked if I was Lucas, to which I always responded, "May the Force be with you."

I raced around the room looking for the producer, but he was gone. The next day I was ready to call him and straighten it out, but realized he'd probably told all his friends Lucas was interested in working with him, so I let it pass. Better he figured Lucas was an asshole who never called, than realize what a fool he'd made of himself over a badly mistaken identity.

Um, if you're still sitting by the phone . . . sorry.

This is not an infrequent occurrence among celebrities and those who are famous because they are on TV. There is an entire industry of celebrity look-alikes in Hollywood. The respectable companies insist that their look-alikes don't take advantage of the mistaken identity. However, one dead-ringer Burt Reynolds look-alike once told me he had an unusual approach to the matter of false identity. When I asked if he adhered to the rules, he said, "Oh, sure, I always tell women I'm not Burt. In the morning."

The worst case of repeated mistaken identity—and the best solution to it—I ever saw took place at a TV station where I once worked.

The station had two platinum blondes on air. The one we'll call Roseann was a reporter, an attractive enough woman, though not beautiful. She bore a slight facial resemblance to the one we'll call Marilyn. (The names have been changed, blah blah blah . . .)

Marilyn, on the other hand, *was* beautiful, and an anchor. She rarely went out into the field to do stories.

Inevitably, Roseann was frequently misidentified in the field by viewers. "Say, aren't you Marilyn? I watch you all the time. I love your work." Occasionally they'd add, "Funny, but you look much prettier on TV."

Incidentally, don't *ever* say that to a TV personality. Also, don't say, "You look prettier in person." Either way you're insulting either her on-camera looks or her in-person looks. And no matter what you think, she won't accept it as a compliment. I mean, you wouldn't say to a neighbor, "You don't look so old when you're outside the house."

Also, don't say things like, "I had no idea you were that short. You look much taller on camera."

These constant public misidentifications of Roseann were merely a nuisance to her at first but eventually became a source of some irritation to a reporter who had her pride and her reputation, and who had been in the market long enough to have her own following.

Sometimes, when she corrected people, they didn't believe her. They thought she was Marilyn trying to deflect attention from herself, or avoid her public. More than once, Roseann had to whip out her wallet to prove that the name on the driver's license wasn't Marilyn.

One day, Roseann came to work in an ebullient mood. I asked why she was so happy, and she explained that she had finally solved her little mis-identity problem.

"What, are you going to let your hair go back to natural?" I asked.

"Nope. I know what to say now when people confuse me with Marilyn. Let's pretend you're someone mistaking me for Marilyn and I'll show you what I do now."

"Okay." I cleared my throat and threw on my most adoring expression, which, if I may say so myself, is pretty durned adoring.

"Oh my God! I *love* your work. And you're beautiful! You . . . you . . . you're Marilyn, aren't you?"

"Yes. Yes, I am," Roseann said with a huge smile. "Now go fuck yourself."

# I Really Should Give Jim Clark a Call

## The Good People and the Strange in TV Land

# I Really Should Give Jim Clark a Call

I should call Jim Clark, I really should. I knew him and worked with him for some six years almost twenty years ago. Haven't run into him since. I was gonna call him when I was working on this book, but he'd probably just deny everything.

Jim Clark is a local reporter in Washington, D.C., has been at the same TV station for some thirty or forty years, and shows no sign of slowing down. He has outlasted a couple of dozen or more news directors, an owner or two, a bunch of news sets, incalculable producers and countless cost cutters.

Fire Clark? It's like the story about Gen. Curtis LeMay, the former Air Force Chief of Staff who was seen standing next to a bomber that was being refueled. LeMay had his customary lit stogie in his mouth. An airman said to one of the general's aides: "Sir, the General better put out that cigar. The plane might blow up."

The aide responded, "It wouldn't dare."

Fire Clark? They wouldn't dare.

Besides, Clark's the best.

I wouldn't want to cross Clark, who is built like a pit bull and may very well be the best television reporter not to work at a network. Not that he hasn't been offered the chance. But Clark didn't need the travel or the struggle to make air every night.

Two things caught my eye about Jim Clark when I started work at my first TV gig at WJLA-TV, Washington, D.C. Clark had already been there for years. Shortly after my arrival, he came storming into the newsroom.

"That's it. It's over. The whole bloody mess is over."

Someone calmed him down to find out what was over.

"News."

"What do you mean?"

"The goddam station has hired a news consultant. News is over."

I had no idea at the time how prophetic Jim Clark was.

Another incident. Jim Clark had done a story on some homeless families freezing on the streets, in need of care.

The story ran, along with a number to call if you wanted to help. The number wasn't the Red Cross or Salvation Army. The number was a direct line to Jim Clark's desk. He stayed at work for hours after the story ran, well out of his shift, on his own time, taking down the names of those who called, making arrangements for the poor to get the blankets and shelter and food.

Jim Clark is under the impression a newsman does more than just report news.

When I worked at WJLA, Jim Clark had the nickname "Madman." I once asked someone, naively, why the nickname. He looked at me as if I was nuts. "Because he's a madman," he finally responded.

But in a good way. There was a method to Jim's madness. He used his temper to get things done. To get the things done he needed to report the news, get it on the air, get the story told.

Like getting an editor to cut his piece.

Jim Clark was never bothered by the occasional shortfall of editors that besets any newsroom. He was the only AFTRA newsman I ever saw who would, in lieu of getting his cutting session scheduled like a mortal human being, could just walk into an editing suite and ask the editor what he was working on. When the editor answered, Jim would say, "Well, you're working on *this* now." Then Clark would eject the tape—a union no-no—and put in his own.

Editors never filed a grievance because, well, it was Clark, and that's what he did.

Jim Clark was as good as or better than most national correspondents. Although he did not want to be bothered with working for a network, he wanted to cover stories of national impact.

When the hostages were released by Iran, Clark and a crew flew to Germany, where the hostages were reunited with their families and given physical and mental checkups.

I remember that Clark broke a couple of stories the national guys didn't get. He even got one story when the assignment was over and he was headed home.

The press had been kept away from mental health experts who had interviewed the returning hostages. Even Clark couldn't persuade them to provide him with a shrink to interview.

Clark was sitting in coach with his shooter when he learned one of the doctors who'd spoken with the hostages was sitting in first class. Grabbing his photog—who like most shooters had his camera with him as carry-on—Clark marched forward to the first class entryway. There he was intercepted by a formidable flight attendant who asked just what the hell did he think he was up to?

Clark gave her a big Irish smile and said, "Good, I'm glad you're here to help us. I'm with ABC, and the president of the network and the CEO of the airline want you to help me interview the doctor." Read that sentence again. It's not really a lie. But without waiting for her to parse his question, Clark blew by her and set up in the middle of the aisle, moving passengers around to get the proper position. The Doc never knew what hit him, and Clark had another exclusive.

To make air that night, Clark had no time to bother with minor details like going through customs. He told his crew to take his bag through, and Clark sprinted for the shuttle from New York to Washington.

What happened to his luggage is now part of the station's mythology. One story has it that customs demanded that Clark's luggage be opened and inspected. Reportedly the agent zipped open the bag, looked in, saw some kind of undeclared contraband and looked up at the hapless cameraman. The cameraman shrugged his shoulders and said, "It belongs to Jim Clark." The agent then reportedly said, "Oh, Jim Clark! Why didn't you say so?" zipped up the luggage and they were on their way.

As I said, that's probably a myth.

Earlier in this book (page 75) is perhaps the most classic of Jim Clark stories—the time he ordered a chopper to hover over the station while he threw down tapes in time to make air. There are other stories equally amazing, some lost to memory. There was the time he ordered his cameraman/driver to keep following a story they were chasing even after the crew car had blown out all four tires. That may be exaggerated, but I don't think so.

Like many of the best reporters, Clark could be a pain in the ass to management and to those who didn't want to tell him the story. In a business where talking back to management is about as welcome as small numbers in a ratings book, Clark has been fearless. And it is one of the truths of television that the Great Ones earn the right to speak up. The array of news directors who put up with his bullheadedness either knew and respected his passion and his abilities or were genuinely afraid to go up against him.

There is not an iota of flash about Jim Clark, but he is an example of all that's good in television journalism. He is no gypsy, moving from market to market. He's stayed where he's belonged while the kids have come and gone.

He'd have fit in in the old Chicago newsroom of *The Front Page* era. In a universe of TV French poodles, he remains a pit bull, and the best damn reporter I ever met.

I really should give Jim Clark a call.

# MacInterview

*In a movie filled with great lines, one of the better ones in*
*Broadcast News speaks well not only to success in the TV*
*industry, but also to success in general. The dim but successful*
*anchor played by William Hurt tells the schlub reporter Albert*
*Brooks of a laundry list of good things happening in his life.*
*What do you do when life exceeds expectations? he asks Brooks.*

*"Keep it to yourself," Brooks answers. Another perfect line*
*written by James Brooks (no relation).*

*Being a TV movie junketeer, at least during its heyday, cer-*
*tainly exceeded any expectations a movie reviewer could have*
*had. A small band of critics and interviewers were sent most*
*weekends to major cities, there to enjoy themselves on the tab*
*and interview stars of upcoming movies. Paid for by the studios*
*themselves.*

*It's fair to let out the secret now because the golden era has*
*passed and junkets, according to my impeccable sources, have*
*become a pain in the neck as often as not. But my memories*
*of junkets are among the fondest of my experience in TV.*

*This particular junket was not my single favorite experience,*
*perhaps not even typical, but it may give you an indication of*
*just how a junket weekend might have gone.*

Unless you are an East Coaster taken against your better judgment
to Southern California for reasons of occupation, marriage or

insanity, you cannot fully appreciate the visceral pleasure of an evening stroll down Chicago's Michigan Avenue in the snow.

Flurries, really, but compared with the smog-cluttered chewable air I've just left in L.A., the flakes are a crisp, fluttering taste of climatological paradise. The only time flakes get in your face in Hollywood is when a screenwriter is being argumentative.

It is November 1992. The street is bustling with Christmas shoppers. Marshall Field's is crammed, Lord and Taylor filled to the brim. I stand outside a Brooks Brothers window looking at the display of impossibly perfect country-squire clothing. If I can't afford them, and certainly have no reason to wear them in Los Angeles, why then am I lusting after the wool sweaters, car coats, wrap-around scarves, and fancy little leather hats men with mustaches and tweed jackets fancy themselves wearing in vintage MG-TD's?

The Mighty Junketeers—that doughty group of media warriors who travel city to city each weekend to bring America a few moments shooting the bull with stars who are hawking their movies—have winged Midwestward for the *Home Alone 2: Lost in New York* junket. It is being held in Chicago in honor of producer/writer John Hughes, who is powerful enough to make Hollywood come to him.

This has been a busy weekend for the junketeers, feasting first on the thoughtful provocations of Spike Lee and Co. in New York City for *Malcolm X*, then flying to Chicago, which is, as you may know, a Toddlin' Town.

To make up for the inconvenience, and buoyed no doubt by the anticipated success of the movie, 20th Century Fox has sprung for first class airline tickets for the Junketeers. Once upon a time, all junkets included a first class ticket. This enabled many to trade it for a pair of seats in coach to bring the spouse or significant other along for the trip.

Because I nailed Spike one-on-one at the opening of his Joint in Hollywood a week earlier, I pass up the New York part of the journey, and fly directly to Chicago for what will be one of the most challenging interviews in all of Junketdom—Mighty Mac.

# Saturday

**9:15 A.M. PST.** Board a United Airlines widebody, take an unaccustomed left turn to first class. I sit next to a guy with a beard and glasses. He is a movie producer. He's done a lot of made-for-TV and some features. We talk movies. I promise to send him my screenplay. He says he's very interested, babe.

**10:30 A.M. PST.** Breakfast is served with real linen, real silverware. The choices are real Kellogg's Special K, or real cheese omelets. I wonder what the heathens are having in coach?

**3:15 P.M. CST.** Land in the Windy City. Cloudy and gray. Say goodbye to Hollywood Producer. I promise to send him my screenplay. He promises to read it. *Ciao.* Exit plane trying to look important.

**3:30 P.M. CST.** Share a cab to the hotel with a producer from one of those Hip, Hot and Happenin' youth-oriented cable entertainment shows. She says she plans to visit some art museums.

**3:45 P.M. CST.** Stuck in traffic. Cabby tells us roads are jammed all winter because of snow, jammed the rest of the year to fix potholes caused by the snow. Says we must love all that sunshine in L.A. Tell him because of the current drought I have to pee five times before flushing. Cabby shuts up.

**3:50 P.M. CST.** Still stuck in traffic. Producer tells me she has friends in Chicago who've been abducted by extraterrestrials. Tell her I have a friend in Boston who can sneeze milk out his nose.

**3:55 P.M. CST.** Producer tells me her piece on Macaulay Culkin won't be fluff. "I have to find a hard-news angle on him." "Why not ask him if he was ever abducted by extraterrestrials?" I suggest. She writes that down.

**5:30 P.M. CST.** Check into the Ritz-Carlton, the first hotel I've seen with its lobby on the twelfth floor. Upon check-in, a Junketeer always determines his daily incidental limit. It's been running about $100–$125 in the big cities. The tab, or *per diem*, which is paid for by the movie company, includes food, booze, laundry and phone calls. No hookers or custom-made suits, thank you. Occasionally the movie company will list what is specifically excluded. On a junket to Las Vegas, for instance, Junketeers were informed that gambling losses were our own responsibility.

**5:35 P.M. CST.** Bellman takes clothes to room. Ask him if they've had any trouble lately with extraterrestrials snatching guests. He says no, but you know, he could be one of *them*.

**5:45 P.M. CST.** Break open the minibar. Hang up clothes. Discover once again that no matter how hard I try, packed clothing comes out of the suitcase looking like something the Swamp Thing has worn for a month. Decide to blow some of Fox's incidental money on a quick press.

**6:30 P.M. CST.** The aforementioned Michigan Avenue stroll.

**7:15 P.M. CST.** Call home. Wife, last seen during 6 A.M. goodbye peck, has a cold. Says eldest son is going out on a date. "Did you get him some . . . you knows?" I ask. "No," she responds, "I didn't know he was going out on a you-know-what, so I didn't get him any you knows." No wonder teens think their parents are complete idiots.

**7:30 P.M. CST.** Junketeers rally on the 12th-floor lobby for the trek to the screening. Fox flacks seem particularly concerned with the Junketeer count. Either the theater will be crowded or they've been having problems with extraterrestrial abductions.

**7:35 P.M. CST.** Spot Hip, Hot and Happenin' Show producer. "How was the museum?" I ask. "I took a nap instead," she says.

**8:00 P.M. CST.** The movie is shown. The theater is jammed with "demographics," the term for the other freeloaders who've gotten free tickets to the movie. Demographics are included because they are expected to love the movie and hence sway Junketeers into a positive review through laughter, applause or osmosis. Same concept as putting a trainer in a tank to glide a newly captured shark around until it learns to breathe in a strange environment.

**10:00 P.M. CST.** Movie ends. *Home Alone 2,* thanks to the demos, filled the theater with laughter, applause and attempted osmosis.

**10:15 P.M. CST.** The Junketeers scatter and I return to my room. Order Caesar salad appetizer, steak, and an amusing but not too presumptuous half bottle of 1989 Cotes du Rhone. The tab is $41.00, not bad for the Ritz. Still well below daily maximum, so I snag two Kahluas and some beer nuts from the minibar.

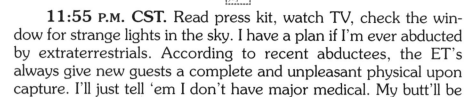

**11:55 P.M. CST.** Read press kit, watch TV, check the window for strange lights in the sky. I have a plan if I'm ever abducted by extraterrestrials. According to recent abductees, the ET's always give new guests a complete and unpleasant physical upon capture. I'll just tell 'em I don't have major medical. My butt'll be back on earth in no time.

# Sunday

**7:00 A.M. CST.** My body still thinks it's on California time (5 A.M.), so I'm a little groggy. This may explain why I brush my teeth with my mousse.

**8:45 A.M. CST.** Junketeers gather at the hospitality suite. Big turnout. All the regulars are on hand, no doubt because of the anticipated box office impact of the movie, and the first class ticket.

**8:50 A.M. CST.** Interview Daniel Stern, who played one of the wacky bandits. Decent interview, nothing spectacular. His hair looks like it came in a kit.

**9:00 A.M. CST.** A Junketeer with the stunned look of cattle headed for execution stumbles into the suite. Has had a disastrous outing with Mighty Mac. "The little pisher didn't answer *anything*."

**9:15 A.M. CST.** Interview director Christopher Columbus. He's so young-looking he makes Macaulay look like Keith Richards.

**9:20 A.M. CST.** Back to the hospitality suite. More slack-jawed junketeers. One wrings her hands. "He doesn't talk!" The Hip, Hot and Happenin' producer is frantic. "How can I do a serious piece if he doesn't talk?" she says. "Why don't you do a Hip, Hot and Happenin' fluff piece?" I suggest. She writes that down.

**9:30 A.M. CST.** Another defeated Junketeer slouches back from his encounter with Mighty Mac. "I asked him, 'What is it like being so powerful that you could threaten not to make another movie there unless everyone on the lot dyes their hair blue?' He didn't answer! He just sat there!" Geez, I think, how could anyone resist a barnburner question like that?

**10:00 A.M. CST.** I'm up soon to interview Mighty Mac. More Junketeers return with more warnings. I'm not worried for two reasons. One, I'm an idiot. Two, I have a boy one year older than the twelve-year-old Culkin. I know the secret to questioning kids that age: bring lots of questions. If they don't like or understand a certain question, they won't answer it; most will just stare at you. Keep asking new questions till they get one they like.

**10:05 A.M. CST.** Ushered into Macaulay's interview suite. Mac is taking a break. One of the camera operators says, "He doesn't give very long answers. He's been getting some dumb questions. One guy asked him why he doesn't dye everybody's hair blue." Briefly wonder if I should call him Macaulay, Mac, or Mr. Culkin. Decide on Macaulay.

**10:07 P.M. CST**. Macaulay enters. He's a kid. He has very prominent lips. I will get five minutes from the moment I hear the word "speed" (which means the cameras are up and running). I speed all right—through 52 questions, by actual count, an average of one question every 5.7692308 seconds, including "Are you married?" and "What's the capital of Idaho?"

Hey, I'm desperate. But then I stumble into some good fortune. I ask Macaulay if he'll do the Scream (made famous in the original *Home Alone*). He shakes his head and gestures to his throat, which either means he doesn't want to strain his voice, or he's choking on a Pop Tart. At this point, I don't care. "Okay, how about if *I* scream?" He nods approval, I scream, and he becomes a director. "Louder," he demands. I scream again. "Louder!" I scream louder. "Not loud enough!" I unleash my loudest scream. Mac gives me an "okay" sign and flashes that five-million-dollar-plus-a-percentage smile. I exhale. I've got something I can use. As I'm leaving his suite, hotel house dicks are arriving. I'll leave it to others to explain.

**11:15 A.M. CST.** Interview producer/writer/Midwest Movie Mogul John Hughes. He looks about as un-Hollywood as one can look, more like a Boston banker about to turn down your loan.

**11:30 A.M. CST.** Do interview with stunt coordinator Freddie Hines. He walks into room as Mac walks out. "How ya doin', Bonehead?" Hines says to Mac. They trade high fives and hug. So *that's* what you call him.

**12:15 P.M. CST.** Cab back to the airport.

**3:00 P.M. CST.** Knockin' back the free hooch in first class. My server, Keith, hands me my first class meal selection menu. The entrees are lobster salad, chicken with mushrooms, and filet mignon. "We only have filet left," Keith informs me. "Got any Special K?" I ask.

**4:15 P.M. PST.** Land at LAX. From wheels-up to touch-down, the junket has taken thirty-one hours. From it, I will get a four-minute piece to be used on a Christmas special. The focus of the piece is about how difficult Macaulay Culkin is as an interview. With music, spectacular Hip, Hot and Happenin' editing, and the Macaulay-as-director ending, the piece works so well it's run separately on the news.

# Know Which Way
# the Wind Blows

It was a perfect day when Louie Allen died. Just the sort of low humidity, blue sky, shirtsleeve day a weatherman would want for his chariot ride up yonder.

Louie Allen made me want to be a TV weatherman. He was the top Washington, D.C., weatherman in the sixties, back when I was a mere froth of a lad. It was Louie who told us no school tomorrow because the low creeping up the coast would provide the moisture and the cold winds sweeping in from the northwest would keep the temperature below freezing. I decided early on I would be a TV weatherman, just like Louie Allen.

Louie made weather forecasting fascinating in a fascinating place for weather. Washington was a bitch to forecast. A degree of temperature difference could turn a forecasted foot of snow into a half-inch of rain, and a change of those always-mysterious "steering currents" could drive the whole mess out to sea and leave the area high and dry. That meant there *would* be school tomorrow.

It was the kind of weather too close for a sane man to call. But Louie called it, and got it right more often than not. When he was wrong, he'd explain what happened, and why Mother Nature always had the last word. Even a disappointed schoolkid could forgive that.

Louie drew you in to the process of weather and weather forecasting, made you feel a part of it. He did not talk down to viewers, nor find refuge in showy technobabble. There was no flash and dazzle to Louie. He never played to the room or pretended weather wasn't important. He didn't tell jokes and chitchat with the anchor. But he was great TV. You liked him and loved that he loved his job. He couldn't hide it. He was a weatherman first, a TV guy second.

So I wanted to be like Louie. I wanted to be a TV weatherman. I told my Mom. Mom cut my legs out from under me with eight well-chosen words:

"You have to know science to do that."

Back to the drawing board. Still, I've always retained my fascination with weather, which is why I remember that it was a perfect day when Louie Allen died.

I knew Willard Scott when he was working in Washington before he went to the *Today* show. If I'd known there were people like Willard who could become TV weathermen, I might well have ignored my Mom's warning. Willard didn't know science. Willard was always larger than life on the air—and off—a high-energy, funny, huge man with little or no pretentiousness to him. Sometimes Willard forgot to wear his toupee on the air. And he cheerfully admitted that his forecasts came from the weather service and he didn't have a clue.

And he was funny. For years in Washington, Willard was one half of the "Joy Boys of Radio," a hilarious drive time team that also included Ed Walker, who later became the first blind talk show host in television.

Willard's act was being funny and high energy, and bringing out the pies and cakes his fans sent him. He was very good at that, and soon he was dragged from Washington to New York to become a star. Eventually, the tug of his Virginia farming roots brought him home.

Before Willard left for the big city, he passed on an important lesson about a new TV gig: "Pay no attention to what you see me do at first. I don't want to scare anybody. I'll be normal to let people get familiar with me before I go into the act."

Willard might have acted the fool at times, but he's no dummy.

When I worked in Boston, I had the questionable fortune of being assigned a space next to Harvey Leonard's weather office. (I had been moved out of the main newsroom when the station began to use it as a news backdrop and deemed me too ugly to be seen out of context.)

Then, as now, one of Boston's most respected meteorologists and TV weathermen, Harvey had two passions in life—weather and the Boston Celtics. Harvey, who treated an occluded front with the respect and admiration due a visiting diplomat, had no such compunction about NBA referees, Celtic opponents, the gods of fate or the way the ball bounces.

Harvey would spend his evenings hunched over his weatherstation with one eye on the weather and one eye on the tube, watching the fate of his beloved Beantown team. He might as well have been in the front row at the Gahden, screaming, unleashing shouts of joy, calls of alarm, strings of curses and calling for the thunder of the gods to rain down and smite the lowly referees who called a charge instead of an obvious blocking call that even *my grandmother could see!!!!!*

Whenever the Celtics played and yours truly was trying to peck out a review on deadline, Harvey, an otherwise decent man, was nevertheless the biggest, noisiest pain in the ass I'd ever known.

I became an entertainment reporter instead of a weatherman. I did the weather on air just once, and my inspiration was less Louie Allen than George Carlin's Hippy Dippy Weatherman. It was April Fool's day when I was given my shot on the noon weather.

I started off seated at the anchor desk, where I noted that the regular weatherman was off, but that he'd briefed me thoroughly, wished me luck and given me a big pat on the back before I went

on. As I walked to the weather set, the camera picked up the "kick me hard" sign taped to my back. Funny stuff, no?

I then noted "there's a large high over Los Angeles, but as near as we can tell it has nothing to do with the weather," and it went downhill from there. There were 22 calls about my performance—the most I'd ever gotten. Half thought I had done a fine job, incorporating humor and irreverence into a normally dull slot. The other half suggested I should be taken outside the studio and shot. Several volunteered to help out.

Despite my continuing interest in weather, I've never really enjoyed the Weather Channel. Every time I tune in, it seems it's either in commercial or giving us the update on the weather in Murmansk. At the point of a gun, I could not name a weathercaster on the Weather Channel. The forecasters, although they seem to know their stuff, have an unmistakable vanilla flavor.

There seem to be new ones added and old ones departed every time the jet stream moves, and no one has—or is allowed to show—any star quality. The presenters are as bland as weather is not. Not a Wacky Wally or Wallina among them.

Like most other channels caught in the crush of narrowcasting, the Weather Channel has been trying to find its place in the new cable pantheon. So, when it was announced they were getting in the business of hour-long weather specials, I dialed in.

The new show is called *Atmospheres*, and it debuted the night a horrific ice and snow storm hit the East Coast. So instead of covering a major breaking weather event at 8 P.M. Eastern Time, the Weather Channel presented two amiable, casually dressed co-anchors in a studio talking about surfing in Australia, how to avoid melanoma, and what the heck's the deal with all those barrier reefs disappearing?

One of the hosts, the relatively effervescent Mish Michaels, teased the upcoming surfing footage thusly: "Some of the pictures we have are so cool and so spectacular you feel you're hanging ten yourself."

Hmmm, sounds like the Weather Channel is a-huntin' that youthful demographic that advertisers covet. It may also have been a dig at her partner, Jack Cantore, who went all the way to Australia to report the piece but didn't surf. ("Even though I didn't get to hang ten with the guys," Jack said in the documentary, "those great pictures made me feel like I was right there.")

While in Australia, Jack managed to remove his shirt—to be checked for melanomas—and interview the dullest surfing experts in captivity. (The melanoma specialists were as dull as you might expect, but who wants a wacky melanoma specialist?) Cantore did find one surfer who said, "You get out of the water [after surfing], and an H-bomb could drop on you—you wouldn't care."

*Atmospheres* fell well short of the kind of first-rate documentaries one sees on Discovery Channel—even the VH-1 and E! Fallen Star Specials. It managed to bury the lead several times. They certainly conveyed no particular sense of crisis about the depletion of the ozone in the Southern Hemisphere. This, despite reporting that it had led to an epidemic of skin cancer all over down under and that Australians are now urged to stay out of the sun completely at midday.

There was also mention of, but no sense of urgency to, news that coral reefs such as the Great Barrier Reef are hypersensitive to ocean temperature change and may be doomed by global warming. I'm not asking for breathless "We're all gonna die!" reporting, but a sense that what they were reporting could adversely affect our lives would have been appropriate.

The Weather Channel has managed to adapt some lame tease techniques, though, to keep folks tuned in. At one break, the audience was asked: "Did Typhoon Steve hit Australia in 1990, 1995 or 2000?" Folks were ordered to stick around for the answer and, of course, everyone was invited to log on to their web site.

As this is the Weather Channel and not the Game Show Network, one has to wonder just how educated they think their audience is. Example: Just before a break, Mish noted: "In Australia, the seasons are backwards, at least to us." Jack hopped in. "We'll explain when we come back." Duh, izzit cuz their calendars are upside down?

But the biggest trouble with this show is that it is on at all.

Weather freaks should be able to tune in the Weather Channel and see some schlub out in a parka skidding along the ice, not some putz a half a world away talking about the spirituality of hanging ten. Where's Louie Allen when you need him?

# Sunny, with a 100 Percent Chance of Falling Weatherman

A station where I worked once brought in a country boy to do weather. In addition to being a weatherman, Weatherman Sam had a black belt in karate.

The station promoted that fact before he debuted. "What has being a black belt got to do with my ability to do the weather?" Weatherman Sam asked me, all wide-eyed innocence. "How'd they come up with that?"

"I don't know, Sam," I answered. "These promotion schemes are created by mysterious wizards using boiling kettles, incantations and the eye of a newt."

Sam had another problem—his hair.

He'd started going bald at a young age. Instead of a hairpiece, instead of living with it, Sam chose hair plugs. This solved his problem—temporarily. Unfortunately, his real hair was still scampering out of Dodge. Sam was left with an ever-widening moat between the castle of new plantings and the retreating ringlet of original issue. Sam had to weave a comb-over and a comb-under together to look presentable

Sam might have been wise to use the ease-into-it approach that had served Willard Scott so well. But his very first night on the air he came out of the slot all folksy charm, and by the time the switchboard melted down there had been some 500 calls of complaint. There had never been anything remotely resembling that before.

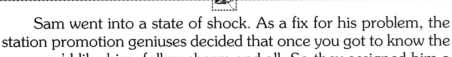

Sam went into a state of shock. As a fix for his problem, the station promotion geniuses decided that once you got to know the guy, you'd like him, folksy charm and all. So they assigned him a ratings sweeps series designed to help the city get to know the guy. (Incidentally, I got to know him, and he *is* a great guy.).

Logic would dictate that Sam do a series displaying the knowledge he'd gained earning a degree in meteorology, show that he knew his stuff. I dunno, "Sam goes to local schoolrooms and tells kids about weather" might have been nice. Instead, the rocket surgeons stirred their caldron of newt eyes and decided the best thing to do was to fling Sam out of a perfectly good airplane. In retrospect, they might have been trying to kill him. They almost did.

Weatherman Sam was assigned a first-person reporter-involvement series about learning how to parachute. Sam took his ground school lessons with cameras recording every move. The series was put on the schedule, and Sam made his first jump.

*Keeeeerrrrrrrrsplaaaaaaattttttttttttt!!!!!!!!!!!!!!*

Sam hit the ground and turned one of his legs into spaghetti. Compound fracture. End of series. Sam did the weather for the next few months on crutches, which might well have earned him more sympathy than the series itself.

Unfortunately, the botched introduction of Sam to the city had already done its bad voodoo, and Sam was considered damaged goods. His stay was a short one, but there was a happy ending. He moved to a folksier clime, where his charm and meteorological skills were a perfect combination.

# Once in Love
# with Greta

I can tell you the exact moment I fell in love with Greta Van Susteren. What I can't tell you is why it took so long. The heart is a fickle organ.

It happened on December 13, 2000, a day better remembered as the one on which Al Gore finally gave up his fight for a presidency honestly snitched by George W. Bush, with the help of the Supremes, the First Governor Bro, Katherine "Maybelline" Harris and the fine election system of the People's Democratic Banana Republic of Florida.

The night before, I had tried to tape *The Daily Show,* my primary source for political information. Instead I hit buttons that erased half my *Smackdown* collection and apparently launched some sort of missile at Indonesia. I'm making progress with my VCR, though. I solved the blinking "12:00" problem, and you can too. Just remember to check your VCR for the correct time only at midnight or noon.

The following morning I carved out time from my busy schedule (write Aunt Tilly next week, feed the carp tomorrow), to watch the rerun of *The Daily Show.* A short few moments into the show, Jon Stewart interviewed Greta, a woman known primarily as the co-host of the CNN program *Burden of Proof* until the post-election brouhaha increased her visibility. A lot of potential viewers thought *Burden of Proof* was a CNN show about blowing the lid off watered-down bourbon scams.

Oh sure, I'd seen the saucy little wench a couple of times on CNN. It seemed she'd been occasionally—how shall I put it?—remiss about such job-related TV matters as makeup and combing of hair. I'd thought her face pleasant enough in repose, but it always seemed that one thing or another was causing her to screw it up in deep thought or passionate discourse. She could be snippy while arguing a legal point with great emphasis and flouting the fact she was smarter than you or I.

In short, I did not find her particularly noticeable. She was smart, yeah, sure, but women smarter than me are a dime a dozen. What I wanted to see was a spark, something that said she was not only smart, but a smart woman, not just a lawyer with boobs.

I was unprepared for her appearance on Jon Stewart's show. For one thing, someone had slapped a coat of makeup on her, and had applied lipstick, something that until that moment I'd more expect to see on Sam Donaldson than Greta.

And that's when I noticed her mouth. With the fiery red outline on her lips now visible, suddenly her off-kilter grin was no longer a liability, but an asset. My God, I thought I was looking at Ellen Barkin in *Sea of Love.*

Stewart, who is not only a comedic genius, but obsequious to guests, poured it on thick to Greta, and suddenly that mouth burst into a broad smile and my heart skipped a beat.

Jon teased her about not getting enough sleep and she teased him back, and for an instant, I thought I saw her throw her kempt hair provocatively. Stewart was eating out of her hand, as was I.

He flirtatiously congratulated her on her new show, congratulated her on her work. She flirted back at him and I felt the long-forgotten pangs of jealousy rip through my churning gut like a mako shark rips though a school of monkfish. (Hey, kids! Great writing is in the specifics.) All those times she had been on *Burden of Proof* she'd used her mind to make her points. And to think, she had all these feminine wiles in reserve. How unfair it might have been if she'd unleashed them.

But now, my little kitten was purring and I was in pain. She smiled, she even appeared to blush at the cascade of compliments Jon passed her way. She moved with grace and fire, readjusted those legs that go on forever. No legalease was coming out of those lips this day. This was the seductress I think we all suspected, in our seething subconscious, lay within.

And so this little minx of mediation, this lovebird of litigation, this hot little jalapeño of jurisprudence was revealing for the first time the well of femininity that lay deep inside her.

Again my heart leaped like a gazelle leaping over a shorter gazelle. I plotted. I planned. But then, a few moments later, my passion was snuffed like a Marlboro squenched up in that metal thingy that's at the top of a car ashtray.

I saw it. How could I have missed it? A rock the size of Nebraska on her marriage finger. My litigious lynx of love, how could you forsake me?

Okay, she's married, and so am I, and I know if I ever met her I'd say something smooth, like, "So, Greta, do I come here often?" She must remain my fantasy woman. So no one tell her— or my wife, for that matter—about this little peek inside my Diary of Might-Have-Beens, okay?

"Greta . . ." Say it soft and it's almost like praying.

"Van Susteren . . ." Say it loud and it's, well . . . it sounds kinda Germanic, doesn't it? Or maybe from one of the Alp countries, like the Von Trapps.

The important thing is, now my little butter squash has her own show and will be available to my eyes twice a day. Life is good again.

# Excuse Me, Where'd You Get Those Ugly-Ass Shoes?

A woman sat next to me on a flight from LAX to New York. I was in my favorite spot, my "poor man's first class" location, the exit row. The woman was a mid-forties, light-skinned African-American. Not a knockout—but then I'm no catch myself. We nodded our hellos, produced our magazines and got ready to spend the rest of the flight in our own cocoons.

After takeoff, a flight attendant hooked her finger at me.

"Do you know who you're sitting next to?" she whispered when I entered her galley.

"If that's Madonna, she's gone too far in the makeover department," I said.

Smartass answer—but since I was sitting in an exit row, and was hence an unsworn member of the flight crew, I felt a kinship with the rest of my airborne homies, my cross-country posse, and believed I had the right to crack wise.

I know I should leave this angle to standup comics, but just when the hell did people sitting in the row by the emergency exit get drafted into the flight crew? You ever read the pocket card about the rights and responsibilities of the exit row door opener? There's a whole page of qualifications and disqualifications written in fluent gobbledygook. For instance, you're disqualified if you have "an indiscernible condition that might cause the person harm if he or she performed one or more of the applicable functions listed above."

Excuse me? I've never had to "lift out, hold, deposit or maneuver objects the size and weight (31–52 lbs.) of over-wing exit doors." How the hell am I supposed to know if I have an "indiscernible condition" that might prevent me from doing that?

How will I know until the time comes if I'm able-bodied and willing to "guide, lead or otherwise help" others, including the halt, the lame, passengers with small children and anyone else who may need a little extra time to get off a burning airliner?

Back to our story, already in progress.

"She's an O.J. juror," the flight attendant told me.

You remember O.J. Simpson. Great running back. Did a little acting and broadcasting. Hertz commercials. Then he murdered his wife and killed a waiter. Let me rephrase that: after being tried and found not guilty of murdering his wife and killing a waiter, he has spent every waking moment since trying to find the real killer or killers on golf courses around the country.

So while O.J. got off on the criminal charges because of a technicality (the jury was nuts), he was ordered to pay Nicole Brown's estate and Ron Goldman's father $33.5 million after a subsequent civil trial. That trial had ended about a week before my flight. Although the immediate frenzy of post-trial interviews had ended, this juror in the civil trial was going to New York to be on the weekend *Today* show.

By now, O.J. is pretty much a tragic footnote, but a few things that the juror said made an enormous impact on me and I feel are worth passing on.

- In the jury's deliberations, the range of the financial settlement swung between nothing at all to $100 million.
- "He essentially decapitated her," the woman said.
- It hadda be the shoes, she said. Those "ugly-ass" shoes that O.J. claimed he never wore but which appeared on his feet in a newspaper photo were key evidence to her. (Imprints from those rare shoes were found at the murder scene.) To fake the Bruno Magli shoe photos, she told me, it would have been necessary for the conspirators to go door to door and collect each and *every* one of the old newspapers that showed O.J. in some

other shoe, plus clean out every library or database of every copy of the paper. A rather complex, clumsy and all but impossible scenario, the woman felt.

- The woman said she had enough spare time during the trial to watch television—but she and the other jurors had been ordered not to watch news or any Simpson-related programming. Because she had a master's degree, she was smart enough to program her VCR to Discovery, PBS and the History Channel. Did the clock on her VCR tell the correct time? I asked. Of course, she replied.
- She did not watch the questioning by the attorneys, but more often watched the reactions of family and the defendant while she listened to the questions.
- At one point, the number two lawyer for the plaintiff had tears streaming down his cheeks.
- One day she thought O.J. was sedated.
- When asked about "animalistic behavior," she said O.J. clenched his hands into fists "as big as my head" and put them down between his legs.
- She felt that cops smart enough to conspire the way that it would have been necessary to frame Simpson wouldn't be on the force as long as Van Atter and Fuhrman.
- She did "not want my 15 minutes of fame" for being an O.J. juror.
- The most effective argument that plaintiff's attorney Daniel Petrocelli made, she felt, was: Why would Simpson permit his attorneys to attack the character of Ron Goldman, who was likely a man "who gave his life defending the mother of [Simpson's] children?"
- She didn't want to profit from her selection, she said. (She later did an HBO special called *Juror Number Five*.)
- Like so many in Los Angeles, she worked in show business, mostly in equity waiver theaters as a lighting specialist. She told people she had a part-time gig downtown during the day, and no one guessed the truth, she said.
- During the trial she felt that her life had not been so structured since kindergarten.

- She believed you could assign a dollar value to a lost son. (I do not.)
- The smokers among the jury members, who took outside smoke breaks, had been tipped off that the media had long range mikes on a nearby hotel. So they would tell dirty jokes and shout, "Bite me," in the media's direction.

After an hour of pleasant conversation, a flight attendant said that the captain, upon being informed of a celebrity on the plane sitting in coach, had extended an invitation to her to come and sit in the first class section. We said our farewells and I spent the rest of the flight memorizing my emergency procedures card. Just in case.

# In Radio, Unlike TV, Nothing Can Go Wrong . . . Go Wrong . . . Go . . .

If you're an on-air person in television news, it may be wise for you to learn the ins and outs of radio to prepare yourself for when those first frightening wrinkle lines appear.

Many television people love doing radio, especially longer-format radio, simply because the constrictions of TV don't apply. You may host a single-topic talk show and discuss something for an hour, instead of cramming everything you know into a buck fifteen, including toss and tag. I did newstalk radio part-time in Washington, D.C., for years while also working in television. For the most part, I loved it.

When I learned my TV junket buddy Dana Hersey—a Boston TV institution—had started his own radio show, I decided I should be a guest during a visit to Boston.

Dana had been installed as morning drive-time talk jock on W-Bach, a Massachusetts North Shore radio station known primarily for classical music and a strong signal. Naturally, the boys in creativity decided that the station needed to take advantage of its strong signal, but rather than shift formats overnight, they decided to do it gradually.

Dana was the first experiment.

You should know a few things about Dana Hersey. He has one of the great voices in radio or TV, a basso of the John Facenda variety. Dana has a great sense of humor, willingness to adventure and a familiarity with the grape. I have spent many a late hour with him and consider him one of my very best friends.

Dana's dip into the world of radio had not been particularly smooth. He and his bosses did not always see eye to eye. Some of the morning experiments had gone wrong, horribly wrong. Some things had gone so wrong on the air, they probably caused casual listeners to swerve into the fast lane, slam on the brakes and stop their cars, jamming traffic while they locked the station onto one of their buttons. (There's even a term for that in Boston. It's called a normal commute.)

One morning, Dana had bee trouble. When Dana arrived each morning before 6 A.M., the station was stiflingly hot. To compensate, one day Dana opened a window to his booth, and then left to get coffee. When he returned just before air time, the room was filled with bees, apparently fans of the show who had been heretofore forced to listen through the window. According to Dana, he proceeded calmly with his show while his newsman attempted to shoo the insects out of the room. Occasionally, over Dana's voice, listeners could hear the sound of a rolled up magazine thumping an unfortunate bee.

On another occasion, Dana and the gang attempted a live shot at a country fair. What could be more fun than having an expert teach Dana how to milk a cow. Aside from operating a working breast, Dana's only experience with a similar activity has been removing a pouring spout from a dead bottle of Maker's Mark.

Unfortunately, comes the witching hour and his expert was a no-show. Dana picks up the story from there:

So I grab some guy who looks like an extra from *Deliverance* in the cow barn and I ask him to get me a cow. The guy literally head-wrestles one into a milking station . . . cow's mooing, guy's getting tossed off his feet, dragging the tops of his work boots in the dirt aisle.

I was laughing so hard and trying to explain what was happening that I had to turn my back on him to continue talking. He gets the cow in the milking stall finally, and I bring the news guy over. He's a city boy so I was torturing him all day. I tell him he's about to learn how to milk a cow.

Then I stick the mike in front of the cow-wrestler's face and demand "Now how does he get milk outta this thing?" and the guy takes a vacant one, two, three beat . . . then slurps through his two remaining teeth and says directly into the microphone:

"Yer jest pull their fuckin' tit!"

"Whoa . . ." I caution, "we're on the radio!" But he presses on, "*Pull her tit . . . yank on her tit!!!*" Turns out the guy was mentally challenged.

I just about shit my pants. The news guy has now buried his face into the side of the cow and his shoulders are heaving; he's having convulsions. I realize I should be panicking, but I can't stop laughing and the *Deliverance* guy won't shut up about tits. "*Pull her tit . . . Pull her tit!!!!*" So in order to help the news guy get himself together—and he is *gone*, by the way—and to shut this guy up, I reach down and start yanking on one. So now both the news guy and me are yanking on the cow's tits and milk, milk is going everywhere, and this guy is hootin' and a hollerin' and yelling gibberish. I'm trying to throw back to the studio but the producer has lost it too.

Finally, the barn manager I was supposed to talk to comes into the barn literally at a dead run, somebody must have told him what was happening, grabs the guy by both shoulders and ushers him off. He was pissed I'd done it without him. General manager freaked a little, too. Bad part was I told the producer to kill the [eight-second] delay on the show so I could listen to off-air in my head set.

There's no way I'm going to match that level of madness, and I have no intention of letting Dana or one of his toadies grab my man-breasts, but I'm eager to see my old friend and check out his chops as a radio guy.

When I arrive, I find the studio to be thankfully bee-free. Hersey, with morning face and disheveled hair, is shuffling through his book of spots to be read, shouting, "I'm completely lost," to no one in particular.

I'll sit with him in the studio for a couple of hours, and talk on air and off with other guests. Among those booked: a man who believes coyotes attacked his Jack Russell terrier and now wants a vigilante posse of lawmen and other gunslingers roaming his neighborhood armed to the teeth, with shoot-to-kill orders.

Keep in mind, this guy has seen a grand total of three coyotes, unless of course Boston's answer to Jack Hanna has mistaken three brown mutts for their cousins. Dana asks him to estimate how many coyotes he believes are in the neighborhood, based on this experience.

"Twenty to thirty thousand," the man responds. Well, that makes sense, I figure. I've seen the Three Stooges, and there are certainly more than twenty to thirty thousand of those on the loose, too.

The man complains that local officials have taken the side of the coyotes. His solution to the coyote problem, "I want the police able to kill the coyotes."

A caller says he's been killing coyotes for a long time with his trusty rifle. Dana responds that the only trouble he's had on his land is "deer nibbling his rhododendrons." They live to nibble another day, Dana says.

There are other guests scheduled, too. An Independent candidate running for some office or another—it was early and I can't read my handwriting—is up next, but the news guy will handle his interview. Later, Dana says he knew it was time for the interview to end when he heard his newsman ask, "So, I understand you play the bass guitar?"

Dana is a font of ideas for upcoming programs. He tells the story that's been in the news about the pig that went berserk on an airline. This was a 300-pound porker, called a "human companion" by its owner. The airline allowed it to stay in first class, and the hog generally behaved until the plane landed and the pig refused to depart. It then fought and pooped and generally made itself unwelcome.

Dana tells me tomorrow he's going to call the airline and try to book passage for himself and a baby gorilla.

"Perhaps you could book your milk cow," I suggest.

Dana seems at least as enthusiastic about his new project, for which he is flying to New York this very day. Some 100 or more brand-new radio stations will be made available to listeners with satellite-ready digital radio. Already, Dana says, cars will have that capability in a year or so. The company he will work for believes that by designing a kind of narrowcasting selection of "stations," it can draw listeners away from the local fare. He'll be doing voice-over work for them and more. He'll be in on the bottom floor.

Dana was long a prominent public figure as host of the *Movie Loft* on Channel 38 in Boston before they got dumb and ended it. He tells me he just turned down a chance to host a new version of the show, in favor of his new radio project.

Looks like Radio Killed the Video Star.

# Frogs with Side Pockets

We all remember when the spirit of Br'er Rabbit and Uncle Remus simultaneously channeled themselves through CBS anchor Dan Rather during coverage of the last election, don't we? Rather is a respected and award-winning CBS anchor—despite a few run-ins with the loosely wrapped. ("What's the frequency, Kenneth?")

Recently, the Gunga Dan image had given way to Respectable Dan. His thoughts were clear, his reporting thorough and concise, his place in television history secure.

But then there was the presidential election. Rather blew the call, like everyone else, but had that been all, no one would have noticed. But then there was good old Dan's on-air Good Ol' Boy meltdown.

In the oddest onslaught of bizarre language since Dan Quayle hung up his tights, Rather regaled the CBS audience throughout the coverage with a painful display of forced folksiness.

Included were these gems:

> He swept through the South like a tornado through a trailer park.

> If a frog had side pockets, he'd carry a handgun.

> This race is tight, like a too-small bathing suit on a too-long ride home from the beach.

It's about as complicated as a wiring diagram to some dynamo.

This race is as tight as the rusted lug nuts on a '57 Chevy.

Al Gore has his back to the wall, shirttails on fire with this race in Florida.

Frankly, we don't know whether to wind the watch or to bark at the moon.

Dan Rather is neither nuts nor dumb. Who got all the post-election ink? Dan. Rather's performance reminded viewers that, unlike his overly staid competition, he is a buried landmine that could go off at any time. And isn't that the fun of live TV?

So the thought occurs that some of you may wish to strike that same level of folksiness but can't, either because you weren't born in Texas and hence lack the recessive Folksy Gene, or because you're dumb as a wet mule stuck in a dry gulch. For those of you who lack the folksy chops, worry not. Here's a batch of starter folksyisms to get you underway:

He's got a plate full of pancakes but his syrup bowl's dry.

He's a two-punch document in a three-hole world.

When flyin' pigs swim, he'll still be in the wallow.

They got fewer chances than a sweet 'tater in a cave full of honey bears.

She's got more moxie than a one-eyed hooker at an optometry convention.

He can backtrack quicker than a moose on skates.

He's got a mouth fulla shouldabeens and a pocket fulla weren'ts.

He's stranger than your uncle's jammies on a prize-winning pig.

Tastier than rhubarb pie swiped from Grandma's windowsill.

Sneakier than a skunk oil salesman with a nose full of hickory nuts.

More nervous than a ticklish dog in a room full of turtles.

More gumption than a double amputee at a cow-milking contest.

If life were a soupbone, he'd try to make succotash.

If cheese were butterflies, it's a sad day in Tulsa if the rains don't come.

# Bill O'Reilly Is a Big Fat Windbag

I received an e-mail the other day from an English stickler. Sticklers tend to be old-fashioned people who care about what is right and what is wrong in the language we use and abuse. They tend to dress in tweeds and use words like "whilst." Sticklers are the people who measure the height of the net before an English match and make sure the rules are correctly enforced. Without sticklers, there would be no rules. Without rules, there would be chaos. Without chaos, there is civility. With civility, you get two vegetables and a choice of soup or salad.

Sticklers are a dying breed. Nobody plays by the rules anymore, as a rule. Breaking rules is hip. Sticklers aren't hip. Sticklers are rarely invited to parties, except the annual Stickler Festival, a bash where sticklers from all over the world gather in silence, each afraid to speak for fear of being corrected and ridiculed.

The stickler who wrote to me had seen an article about a new multi-million-dollar contract signed by Bill O'Reilly, host of Fox News Channel's wildly successful show *The O'Reilly Factor* and author of a wildly successful best seller. This was not what the stickler was specifically stickling about. Nevertheless, I think my stickler friend blithely skipped over something infinitely more significant, and nobody likes a blithely skipping stickler.

He failed to note this extraordinary coincidence: Just how difficult was it for Fox to find a guy named "O'Reilly" to host a show called *The O'Reilly Factor*? Huh? Talk about a needle in a haystack. I personally think Bill O'Reilly was in the driver's seat all the way with his new contract negotiations, since *he* knew that Fox knew the chances of lightning striking twice O'Reilly-wise were nil. Fox surely felt it was worth a few extra million clams to avoid having to find another O'Reilly to replace him.

But then, sticklers often miss the big picture while searching · for minutiae. So my stickler friend focused on offensive usage of language in the article announcing O'Reilly's new contract:

> [O'Reilly's] written a fictional novel. His first book, *Those Who Trespass: A Novel of Murder and Television*, is a mystery novel revolving around a string of murders at a fictional news network.

The point of sticklement: a redundancy. Instead of quietly turning it over to the Department of Redundancy Department, the stickler forwarded it to me with these comments:

"Howcum an editor didn't catch '*fictional* novel.' And howcum I bother to ask? And howcum I care? Or do I?"

These are not only the words of a stickler, but the pitiable bleat of a stickler who is losing faith, a Doubting Stickler.

So I sent back this reply:

> Of course you care. I also care that people write fiction novels. Is that the opposite of a *roman à clef*, or non-fiction novel? Where do Tom Wolfe, Thomas Keneally and Anonymous fit into all this? What about the docudrama? Is there a God? And if so, can you get a good haircut in heaven? Why is there phlegm? If you ask someone, "what is rhetoric?" will he answer you, or just assume it is a rhetorical question?

Did I really write that last line, or subconsciously lift it from Steven Wright?

Why am I telling you, the simple reader, all this? Let me rephrase that. Why am I telling you, the reader, all this? Simple. It's a blatant attempt to snag Bill O'Reilly's attention. He's a thin-skinned sensitive soul, like most good Irish. He is more than delighted to use his bully pulpit, his poison pen, or even his woolly mammoth to crush those who would stand up to him. I fully expect, indeed, I *depend on* him to tear me a new one with some roaring screed that calls me liberal, left-wing, gutter slime or perhaps something disparaging.

Bill O'Reilly has used other media himself to make himself a star, and he now kvells as King of the Fox News Channel Hill, at times out-rating CNN's King of the Hill, Larry King. (Another coincidence: CNN finding a man named King to be its "King of the Hill.")

By mentioning O'Reilly in my modest little opus, I'm hoping to entice the big windbag to take the bait and mention my book or me on his show. Hey, he ain't Oprah, but on the other hand his viewers are more likely to be media and political freaks, and hence more inclined to buy my book than some weepy women's novel Oprah might hype.

So, O'Reilly, the ball's in your court, you fat-headed, overrated creep. Go ahead, mention my book on your show. I don't care if you rip it or praise it to the high heavens. Any publicity is good publicity. If you have a hair on your patoot, you'll invite me to appear on your show, where I'll show you how a real Irishman handles criticism, you three-dollar phony.

I'll bet "O'Reilly" isn't even your real name. A good source, whose initials are Matt Drudge, told me your name was originally Jamaal Shareef.

You've got my e-mail and phone number, right, Bill?

# What Did Dubya Do to Dennis?

I interviewed political comedian and satirist Mort Sahl a few years back. Okay, quite a few years back. For those of you too young to remember him, Sahl was kind of the Dennis Miller of his day. Iconoclastic, smart as hell and a brilliant political commentator–satirist. He's still around, but the spotlight has moved on.

Sahl had been pretty much out of the national consciousness for a few years when I spoke to him, although he was still revered by fans of his take-no-shit attitude and brilliant comedic mind.

When I talked to him, I was surprised to hear the rock-ribbed iconoclast name-drop like a Hollywood hustler, including many people who'd been the victim of his acid barbs before. Some of his new best friends, it appeared, were older, successful people, no matter their politics.

After some thought, I realized why. People get into show biz to get laid, the old saw has it, but once famous, it's the seduction of fame that keeps them there.

Becoming famous gets you inside the velvet rope, but it is not a lifetime membership. Some have their 15 minutes and disappear without a trace. Other stay long enough to join the Brotherhood of Celebrity Survivors (BCS). The BCS is that senior group of celebrities who have more in common with one another than with the rabble outside the rope, even if that rabble shares a similar talent, cause or occupation. The BCS knows no political restrictions and asks no questions about the nature of fame, or

151

how you became famous in the first place. Boxers and criminals, movie stars and politicos, comedians and the financially famous (we're talking Trump and Gates level, not run-of-the-mill multi-millionaires) are all welcome.

In the imaginary bar in their imaginary clubhouse, you'll find Oliver North sipping a martini with former Chicago Seven activist (and later California legislator—see how it works?) Tom Hayden; Jesse Jackson and Dr. Ruth at a table with Madonna; Ice-T drinking daiquiris with Martha Stewart; Rush Limbaugh shooting the breeze with Bill Clinton; Richard Hatch and Richard Simmons exchanging recipes for low-fat grubcakes. Elton John singing duets with Eminem.

They all share a secret. They know what it takes and what it means, who had to be stepped on, who had to be dropped, whose ass had to be kissed to get into and stay inside the velvet rope.

When I interviewed Sahl, I asked him what he thought of the upcoming election. Sahl did not favor the Dems nor the Republican newcomer. His man was fellow BCS member, former White House Chief of Staff and staunch conservative General Al Haig. Imagine stretching your arms wide apart. You'd expect to find Haig at the farthest tip of your farthest right finger, and Sahl at the farthest tip of your farthest left finger.

Still, Sahl knew Haig. Sahl supported Haig. And why not? Why shouldn't Mort Sahl find comfort and shared experience and friendship with General Al Haig, who is of his same era and roughly same age? Doesn't Sahl have more in common with those who worked within the BCS system than Rage against the Machine or other commoners?

(Sahl tells the story of the time Haig, puffing away on a stogie, offered Sahl one, noting "They're Cuban." Sahl responded, "My God, General. You are a staunch anti-Communist. How can you do something that supports Castro?" "Support him?" Haig replied. "I like to think I'm helping burn his crops to the ground." Fidel? You know Liz and Rush, don't you?)

Specific ideology becomes less important within BCS. There are, of course, blood feuds between members, but people in the BCS understand that. Civilians never do.

I hadn't thought about Sahl and the BCS for a while until I saw the inauguration eve (January 19, 2001) Dennis Miller show.

It was his second show of this new season. But, as he noted, the last one he would do while Bill Clinton was president, the only president in office since his show debuted.

Now Miller has been no Clinton fan. In fact he's ripped him as viciously and as humorously as anyone. But there was never a suspicion that Miller had serious leanings to the right. He appeared to be a relatively pure iconoclast whose attacks seemed to have less to do with political preference than human folly in general. And if it came to conflict between ideology and comedy, Miller has always known laughs come first.

But Miller's most recent off-season from his show was different from all the rest. He was the famous Third Man in the Booth on *Monday Night Football*. It was a huge leap forward, celebrity-wise. Miller was suddenly no longer a clambering, struggling, failed-talk-show–hosting, cult hero acid-humorist. He was Famous. Cover of *Sports Illustrated* famous. Now Miller was surrounded not by fellow iconoclasts, but by straightforward smashmouth sports people, for God's sake. No crying in baseball, and no irony in football. In football, you see the guy, you hit the guy as hard as you can. The one left standing is "it."

So now Dennis was absorbed deeper into the inner circle of the BCS. He could barely see the velvet rope from his lofty new position. And so the seduction began.

"No need to be nasty, Dennis. You're part of us now. Stop struggling so much. Lie back and enjoy it. You know Dubya, don't you?"

And that was where the surprise came from. Not that Miller didn't like Al Gore. But it was a shock to those outside the BCS to hear that Miller *liked* the idea of George W. Bush as president. "I feel more comfortable with the dumb guy," he said, trying to pass it off as a one-liner.

Come on, Sparky, the guy can't put a coherent thought together. You are the master of convoluted and brilliant compound-complex sentences so profound they not only make the point themselves, but throw in an ironic subtext explaining the theory of evolution and why wildebeest abhor haiku. Dubya, on the other hand, says things like: "Will the highways of the Internet become more few?" And "The California crunch really is the result of not enough power-generating plants and then not enough power to power the power of generating plants."

It would be one thing if Miller welcomed a Bush presidency because he needed fresh fodder for his comedy mill. Letterman admitted that, even trotted out one of his writers who wanted Bush to win because Letterman's comedy staff was "lazy and didn't want to work hard" for the next four years.

But Miller said he was glad Bush won, and he said it without irony. No familiar Miller smirk. He just said he's glad the lying scumbag is gone, relieved the wooden guy didn't win, happy the Republican and his administration is in office.

This is being written shortly after the inaugural, and it is hoped and expected that Miller will come off that attitude before long. As he gets further out of the influence of the good ol' boy conservatism of the jockocracy and falls more under the sphere of his perverse non-BCS writers, I expect Miller will be pounding Bush like Clinton let loose in a roomful of fresh interns, Cha-cha. Miller has probably snapped out of it already.

But that second show was disturbing for other reasons. The low level of energy Miller displayed—the reaction, perhaps, of a Parisian visitor back on the farm? The complete lack of his self-congratulatory cackle—which always struck me as the audible pause of an insecure performer.

This could indicate a newfound sense of confidence, because of his acceptance by his new big-time sports-star people pals. Miller is the kind of guy jocks beat up in high school. And show biz, as Letterman says, is just high school with money. So his late-onset acceptance can lead to new temptations.

But Cha-cha is too bright a bulb to let that lead to his own ruination, and some of the follow-up shows indicated that Dennis was already starting to snap out of it.

Still a long way to go to catch up to self-described Libertarian Bill Maher, who hates all politicians with seemingly equal venom. Maher, instead of growing comfortable in his own celebrity skin, is as irascible as ever, with annual increases of arrogance, cynicism and condescension toward all who disagree with him.

Leno remains the human joke machine. Years ago as a stand-up, he was one of the few comedians to successfully work squeaky clean. (Jerry Seinfeld was another.) Now Leno's monologue is too often a smarmfest, a slew of dirty jokes aimed at the lowest common denominator.

Letterman remains consistently evenhanded. After eight years of constant attacks on Clinton, but usually at a much more sophisticated level than Leno, he is now taking on Bush. One gets the impression Letterman holds Bush in contempt, particularly following his disastrous appearances on the program. Letterman, though entitled, would never be a BCS member.

Jon Stewart wears his liberalism on his sleeve, yet still manages to get off shots at the center, left and right with equal alacrity.

While Leno and possibly Miller appear to be caving in to the twin temptations of ratings and celebrity, Letterman and Stewart have not. Maher doesn't much like anything on two legs that won't go to bed with him. Ironically, it's his man's man crotchety 'tude that makes him still appealing.

I haven't given up on Miller by any stretch. In fact, my entire theory may be a load of crap. I suspect that by the time *The Dennis Miller Show* has finished the 2001 season, and before he goes back to his second year on *Monday Night Football*, Miller will have reverted to his old, cynical, "they're all bums" attitude. But of course that's just my opinion. I may be wrong.

# Andrea Gets the Blues

*When actress Andrea Thompson from* NYPD Blue *left the show, she shocked everyone by taking a job as a TV reporter. This did not sit well with a number of letter writers who let* ShopTalk *know exactly what they thought. I felt compelled to respond.*

While the view is better from a high horse, I think the rarefied atmosphere at such a perch has beclouded the thinking of some *ShopTalk* writers. Well, thank God, or people like me would have nothing to write about, would we?

Today's topic, the rants and raves of some newsies against Andrea Thompson. She's the *NYPD Blue* ex-regular who glommed onto an anchor gig in New Mexico (I *think*, or it could be some other state with sand).

Anecdotally, you could argue Andrea is over-qualified for the gig. I've served with many fine anchorettes in my day, including two who came from backgrounds perhaps more daunting than Miss Thompson's. One was a former Miss America, the other a former actress who had showed her yahas in a teen-oriented flick. Both have anchored at more than one station in the number two market in America and done quite well, thank you. (Although, as this is written, both are on the beach.)

Both have disproved the stereotype that one must be glum and educated to read the news. For what it's worth, I think Dennis Franz would make a fine news anchor too, and his hairy caboose

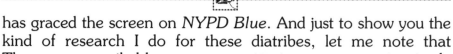

has graced the screen on *NYPD Blue*. And just to show you the kind of research I do for these diatribes, let me note that Thompson unveiled her own superstructure on a recent episode of *Arli$$* on HBO.

"What will she do if (and when) faced with some sort of ethical dilemma in the field?" asked one *ShopTalk* correspondent.

Try this test. Watch *NYPD Blue*, then the late news that follows. Now honestly tell us which has more integrity. Let us know who has more smarts, NYPD exec producer David Milch or Wacky Wally who gives the weather from the local state fair.

And how smart do you need an anchor to be? Why, there's one in L.A. who did an anchor involvement piece and parachuted with the Army's Golden Knights. Crack-crack-crack. Three broken bones. You don't have to be a genius to know it makes no sense to jump from a perfectly good airplane, but it helps.

The biggest argument against Ms. Thompson's intelligence is, how smart can someone be who becomes a TV anchor as her forties loom? (Hasn't anyone briefed Andrea about ageism in TV?) And I know she took her current gig before the report out here in L.A. that female anchors drag down a lot less cash than their male counterparts, but that doesn't speak too highly of her career choice either.

But guess what? Thompson says she wants to do the gig because she believes she can do some good. I'd say that's a better motivation than that of anchors who want to make a lot of money, get the best table in restaurants and sign lucrative hair gel endorsements. (You know who you are. The rest of you, at ease! I know there are many first-rate, journalistically motivated anchors).

And being an actress is hardly a liability. If she can convince me she actually cares about the drive-by she's reporting instead of just putting on the Sad Face consultants recommend, I'd watch her.

If, seconds later, she can convince me she's recovered enough from the trauma of that item to convey honest glee at Fluffy the Kicker Kitten's escape from the garbage disposal, by Gad, she'll be in the big time in no time.

And, last I heard, she's still at work, still doing well, and to everyone who thought it was a temporary gig, I laugh up my sleeve at you.

*Sigh. Now dear Andrea has moved on. Her promotion to CNN anchor re-lit the fire of controversy—and inspired a host of web sites showing her physical attributes.*

# Is This the Best 20-Minute Cassette Ever Shot?

The shooter was having a horrible day. Absolutely nothing was going right. For one thing, it had been snowing all day. That meant he would be miserably cold for the outside stories, and risk pneumonia for stories where he went from slogging around in the cold to overheated rooms indoors. Some years, blizzards hit the Nation's Capital, but not often enough to teach Washingtonians how to drive in them. The roads were a mess.

Then there was the equipment. The equipment didn't like Chester Panzer and his partner George Patterson at all that day. Two stories had been blown out because the camera crapped out or the recorders didn't work, or the cables didn't cable, or Lord knows what else go right. They were on their third camera and hadn't shot a useable frame of tape.

And it *had* to be on Chester's day to shoot. Like many of the two-man crews, Chester and George alternated jobs each day. Today was Chester's day to be cameraman, and George got to lug the big recorder around and do sound. It was 1982, years before the equipment had been miniaturized to the point that one-man bands were the rule.

What a wasted day, Chester was thinking. A wasted day in the snow with equipment that didn't work. Oh, well; you have to take the good with the bad. Chester and his partner were off the clock now. They were given a crew car to take home because they both lived in the Virginia suburbs, not too far from each other.

In the trunk was yet another camera, bench-tested to work, plenty of tapes, and fresh bricks (batteries) fully charged. Today had been a one-story news day. Their first job the next morning would be to get B-roll of the storm's effect in the Virginia suburbs. The area was in the grip of a fully developed blizzard and everyone knew that would be the top story for the next few days. As events turned out, everyone was wrong. There would be a new lead, and Chester and George would be in the middle of it.

But now, a little before 4 P.M., they were stuck in traffic. It was snowing heavily, the wind was blowing, and the roads were being covered and re-covered faster than the plows could clear them. The two men were crawling up the Virginia side of the Potomac River short of the Key Bridge.

They were in the traditional crew car, an off-white, lumbering, fuller–than–full-size Ford Crown Victoria, a massive piece of Detroit metal with rear-wheel drive. This was before microwave technology put almost everyone in vans and SUVs. They hoped that with the equipment in the trunk, the snow tires might maintain enough traction to keep them from getting stuck. But the stop-and-go traffic wasn't helping.

Even though they were off the clock and headed home, they had the radios on. You always keep the radios on. The snow kept piling up, and news people shot pictures of cars crashing, people trudging through snowdrifts, children making snowmen.

The area had all but ground to a halt. Businesses were shutting down early; the radio was filling up with news of canceled meetings and school closings. Government workers had been sent home early, and now their cars were getting caught in the jam of late afternoon traffic. Looks like they'd be there for a while, Chester thought. He glanced across the grass median between the north and southbound lanes of the parkway. The other side was moving, of course; what else could he expect on a day going as badly as today?

Washington's new subway eased a little of the traffic mess, but not much. Only part of it was completed, and the lines that were running put only a small dent in the above-ground traffic. This day, two of the brand-new subway trains would collide, killing three people. Normally, that would be a lead story, but it was only the third lead on this most newsworthy day.

Amazingly, National Airport was still open. Planes were taking off and landing, with breaks every so often for plows to clear the runway. Planes were being de-iced after they left the gates, then lining up for a takeoff that might come much later. It was just before 4 P.M. when a Boeing 737 designated "Palm 90" began its takeoff roll.

Two seconds before the hour, the copilot said to the pilot: "God, look at that thing. That don't seem right, does it? Uh, that's not right."

Palm 90 struggled off the runway, its engine anti-ice in the off position, the plane using only 71 percent of its thrust.

Forty-eight seconds after the hour, the pilot said, "Come on forward . . . forward, just barely climb."

Eleven seconds later, the pilot said, "Stalling . . . we're falling."

At one minute after the hour, the co-pilot said, "Larry, we're going down, Larry . . ."

A second later, the pilot responded, "I know it."

The first radio calls Chester and George got from the station were a little confusing, as they often are. There were reports that a small private plane might have crashed into the Potomac River, near the 14th Street Bridge. Many years before the proliferation of cell phones, there were no immediate on-scene calls to report what had happened.

Not much was being made of it, at first. Police, fire and ambulances were on the way. It would undoubtedly be a sidebar to the snow story when and if they found whatever it was that had crashed through the ice and was sinking in thirty feet of water in the Potomac River.

The crew cars from the station were scattered about the city, none near the accident site. Chester saw the open freeway across the way and reached for his radio. He called the assignment desk. Did they want him to try to get to the scene? A moment's hesitation, and then the go came. They were closest to the scene.

They gunned the Crown Vic and turned onto the grassy median. Chester and George weren't sure they would make it.

There would be the very real possibility that they'd get stuck in the accumulating snow and slick grass between them and the road back to the 14th Street Bridge and the site where the private plane had gone in.

Only now it wasn't a private plane. Now it was an airliner, they were saying. An airliner, taking off from Washington National Airport, had crashed on takeoff and was in the river. There were survivors in the water. Helicopters were in the air; people were on the bridges.

The Crown Vic with the weighted-down trunk spun its wheels and struggled across the median, and Chester and George were soon on the open parkway headed toward the scene of the accident.

Before long they saw the red and yellow lights of emergency vehicles flashing in the distance. They pulled off the parkway onto the grass, near the bridge. Operating on instinct now, the two men rushed to the trunk, Chester grabbing the camera and a fresh brick, George grabbing the recorder, cables, extra cassettes.

There was something happening on the Virginia side of the shore. Firemen and paramedics were gathered helplessly on the shoreline. A woman had survived the accident. A chopper hovered above her; a sling was lowered to her. But she had been in the water too long. She was freezing to death in front of everyone's eyes. She would not be able to stay above the water much longer; nor did she have the strength to grab the sling and be pulled up.

Panzer was in position. He started to roll and began to record what may be the most dramatic and inspiring 20-minute cassette ever made. (At least until every near-death experience would be recorded by the mass of camcorders in the hands of the public.)

"I didn't even know if I was getting anything. I said a quick prayer that the camera was working. We were due to get one that worked."

The woman was going to die. You look at the tape later and you know she was going to die. You can see the life slipping out of her. Chester was recording a drowning, a death made all the more tragic because she was so close to rescue. The firemen, in their heavy yellow protective gear, stood immobile by the shore, not sure what to do. And then, Panzer did something by instinct that would give him the full picture of the drama before him.

He had been tight on the woman. Her expression, her agony, the futile struggle to grab the sling, her eyes growing deader by the moment . . . her death moments away. He had it in his lens.

"You're supposed to shoot with your other eye open," Panzer said later. "A lot of people don't. You're focusing hard on what is going on in front of your eye on the lens, and sometimes you just close the other eye.

"I don't know exactly why I went wide when I did."

You view the tape and you see the shot widen out suddenly, almost a snap-zoom, nothing smooth, nothing meant to be seen as all one shot, but it settles not an instant too soon. You see, moving quickly from the left, an onlooker, a civilian, a man who had stopped to see the drama. Lenny Skutnik, age 28, plunged into the water and began a frantic swim to the woman.

Chester had it all in his lens as Skutnik threw his arm around the woman and tried to return to the shore.

Chester captured the firemen, shocked into action, as they stumbled into the freezing water to help bring the woman and Skutnik to safety in the last few feet. It is extraordinary footage.

Panzer shot up the rest of the cassette as the woman was put on a stretcher and the fireman desperately tried to warm her and get her to a hospital. When he showed me the cassette, he noted some footage that might have been ignored.

"There was this one fireman who had this long scarf. You could tell it was something special to him. I don't know, maybe his mother made it for him or something. Now watch here."

I watched as the fireman followed the rescued woman up the hill on the stretcher, unwinding his special scarf from his neck as he went.

When they reached the top of the hill, just before they put the woman in the ambulance, he put the scarf on her, tucked it around her neck. Just a simple act of kindness, lost in the drama of footage that would be shown around the world again and again.

I remember watching the video for the first time. The other stations had been on the air first, from locations on the bridge. Channel Seven was late. But when Panzer's footage was couriered back to the station and rolled on to the air, it was far and away the best.

I've lost track of Chester and George over the years. But I doubt they've ever had so extraordinary a day. Afterwards, George would joke that he'd become a piece of TV trivia: "Who was doing sound when Chester shot that amazing Air Florida footage?"

# Then Something Went Wrong, Terribly Wrong

## Thirteen True Stories about the Worst That Can Happen

*The late Kermit Shaffer called them "bloopers." They are the mistakes on the air that give us an unexpected laugh. In this section, we go a little beyond that, including some incidents where things went wrong, terribly wrong, or just ridiculously wrong, behind the scenes. All but one incident occurred at places where I worked, either while I worked there, or in the annals of history. In most cases, I've omitted names to avoid embarrassing the person who succumbed to human foibles. As most of these yarns come from my memory or that of others, there may be a slight exaggeration or two. We open with a legendary prank played on a stubborn anchor.*

# The Good News Is, We're Number Two

When TV newscasts began they were much simpler. Frequently, you just got a guy from radio and stuck him in front of the camera in a studio. There, he read his copy into the camera. No co-anchor, no desk, no film, no tape, no slides, no chair, no commercials. Just a guy standing in front of a camera reading the news from copy in his hand.

In those days, there was a tradition at the station. Every new guy had to be cracked up *on air*. Any technique, including setting his copy on fire or hiring a hooker to do her magic just out of camera range, was fair play.

One dour new guy could not be cracked up under any circumstances. Rock solid. A complete pro. Naturally, the techies took this as a challenge. So, one day, they came up with *The Plan*.

Here's how it went. The guy started reading the news. It was a fifteen-minute straight read, no breaks. Once he started, one old-timer went into action. Standing just off camera, he spread a newspaper on the floor. The newsreader noticed, but he was not distracted and plowed onward.

Next, the techie slowly got one of the large rolling platforms they use to change overhead lighting in the studio. He rolled it a few feet away from the reader, right by the camera, just above the newspaper.

At this point, the reader was curious and a bit nervous, but flush with his earlier successes, he seemed confident to the point of smugness.

Then the techie slowly climbed the stairs on the platform, got to the edge closest to the reader and the newspaper. He turned away from his victim. He had his attention now as the reader wondered what was in store for him.

Then in a quick movement, the techie unbuckled, lowered his pants and underwear, took careful aim at the newspaper and— bombs away, Number Two style.

It worked.

# Yesterday's News

Years ago, weathermen were often picked primarily for their ability to hold their liquor between newscasts. Before the era of real-time satellite imagery, computer graphics and StormCast 5000 gimmickry, the weatherman didn't have much to do between the early news and the late. So, many went out to drink dinner and returned to do essentially the same weather service forecast they'd done for the six.

The lubricated weathermen worked hard to overcome the slowed movements, the careful enunciation, the unfocused eyes that give away an inebriated man pretending to be sober.

One particular night, though, one weatherman miscalculated his alcoholic intake and was unqualified to do the late news, possibly because he was unconscious. His friends feared he'd be fired if management found out, and figured the best thing to do would be to re-rack his forecast from earlier that night.

A harried producer ordered the tape dubbed off and sent to the control room to be run at eleven. A good plan—almost. Unfortunately, the tape that was dubbed was from a year earlier. The report that ran at eleven on that beautiful star-filled summer night contained warnings of brutish thunderstorms, ominous funnels, high tides, low-level flooding, hail the size of Studebakers, plus a rain of cats and dogs, chickens and muskellunge.

As the tape ran, no one at the station was paying attention. The weathercaster's friends might have pulled it off, were it not for a trickle of confused phone calls, including one from the mayor's emergency center.

And the weatherman? He was allowed to keep his job, albeit with a large chew taken out of his caboose.

# If the Name Don't Fit, You Can't Acquit

It was well before the O.J. Simpson trial would begin. I was getting ready to go to work one morning when I got a call from one of the reporters at the station.

"Johnnie, how are you?" he asked.

"Great. And you?"

"Pretty good. Say. I have a question, maybe you can answer for me."

"I'll try."

I am nothing if not cooperative. And it wasn't the first time someone from work had called about a piece of movie trivia or to find out if I knew some recently arrested star's agent.

"Thanks, Johnnie. Listen, I've been looking over the lawyers O.J. has so far, and none of them strike me as a real good criminal trial attorney. I'd like to ask you some questions on camera about whether or not you are considering joining the team."

"Well, actually, I think you have the—"

"We'll come to you," he interrupted. "Just tell me where you'll be in about an hour and I'll have a camera set up there. It won't take more than five minutes."

"Well, if you insist, but—"

"I'm on my way. Where will you be in an hour?"

"Where are you standing now?"

"In the newsroom, why?"

"By your desk?"

"Yes."

"Good. Set the camera up two desks down from you. I'll be there in an hour."

"What?"

"It's my desk, so it's real convenient."

A pause. Then . . . "Cork?"

"Yes. You've called John Corcoran, and as of this moment I have no plans to defend O.J."

"Those motherfuckers at the [assignment] desk gave me the wrong number!"

"Does this mean you won't be interviewing me?"

Footnote. I don't recall if he eventually got the interview with Johnnie Cochran. But he had the scoop.

# You Wouldn't Tease Me, Would You? Part 1

The station ran a newscast each night, followed by a late movie. One of the anchors, an African-American woman, was not universally beloved by the staff at the station, a number of whom she treated badly.

As this was quite a few years back, there were no fancy produced promos for upcoming local shows, just a slide and an audio cart. Occasionally they got mixed up. Which might explain why a photo of the anchor ran with the following cart:

"Tonight, be sure to watch *The African Queen*."

# Has Anyone Seen My Surgical Gloves?

It was a children's show. A live, local children's show, rarely done anymore. The director was a gruff news type. One morning the scheduled guest on the morning show was a monkey. A real live monkey—or at least it was when it entered the studio. The name of the monkey is lost to history—to my history, anyway. Let's call him "Mr. Monkey." Apparently, be it from nervousness or as a bad reaction to the hot lights, the monkey keeled over dead during the commercial break before being introduced.

The host of the show panicked. "What do we do?" he asked the floor manager.

Mr. Monkey's owner burst into tears.

"What will I do without Mr. Monkey? What am I supposed to do?"

The floor manager, also upset by the sudden demise of Mr. Monkey, got on his intercom and informed the show's director of the disaster. "Oh my God, Mr. Monkey just died! What should I do?"

The director gave it a few seconds of consideration, realized he was about out of commercials and had to throw back to the studio or dip to black. His reply has become legendary:

"I don't care if you stick your finger up Mr. Monkey's ass and wiggle it like a puppet, but we're coming back to you in five seconds."

# A Meal Is a Meal Is a Meal

I had heard the rumor. One of the shooters at the station had once allegedly scarfed down a special meal intended for the very person he was supposed to interview. The shooter was setting up early in the interviewee's hotel room when room service delivered the meal. The interviewee had not yet arrived. Under the Unwritten Media Law that any food within 25 yards of a media person on assignment is fair game, the shooter reportedly wolfed down all the chow before his interviewee and the reporter even arrived.

The shooter was assigned to me for a story and I decided to find out.

"Is it true?"

"Of course not. Absolutely false. I did not eat his meal."

"Did you eat any of it?"

"What kind of question is that?"

"One you didn't answer. Did you eat any of his food?"

"Well, the salad looked really good. So I took a bite of it. It was a big salad. A dinner salad."

"You ate his salad?"

"No! Aren't you listening to me? You know. Some . . . Most."

"What about the rest of his meal?"

"Okay, pretty much all of his salad."

"You ate all his salad?"

"I had no choice. That's what he ordered. Been up to me, I'd have ordered a steak. Not a dinner salad. I ate a roll, too. And some butter."

"I also heard you drank his wine."

"False. Not true. Definitely not true."

"You didn't drink his wine?"

"I had a sip."

"Just a sip?"

"A glass. Maybe two. It was a small glass. I definitely remember I left some wine in the bottle."

"But why did you eat the food and drink the wine?"

"It was there, wasn't it?"

"Good point."

The victim? The Rev. Jesse Jackson.

# You Wouldn't Tease Me, Would You? Part 2

Perhaps as a result of the *African Queen* slide and cart blooper, the anchor started doing her teases live on camera shortly after the incident. She preceded the spots with a self-applied makeup touchup at her anchor seat. A floor manager cued her into the break, but one night either he was out of the loop, or the control room surprised everyone and cut to her early.

If you're watching at home, you hear the familiar recorded lead-in to the tease and the next thing you see is the anchor rapidly powdering her face while making those odd faces women make when they powder their face. She checked a hand mirror approvingly, then back at it. After a few moments of this, the puff froze and the anchor called offscreen: "What?" She appeared to listen intently for a few seconds, then her face turned to cold steel as she warned the off-camera presence: "I better not be, or I'll *kill* you."

# Some People Should Not Reproduce

So far, the parties in these stories have been kept anonymous to avoid embarrassment. While the following incident might be considered an on-air blooper, the behavior of the key player turned what might have been a disaster into an event that most people missed completely. But videotape of the incident was shown over and over again in the station and one woman's coolness under fire became the stuff of myth and legend.

Renee Poussaint was an anchor at WJLA-TV, Washington, D.C., a classy and brilliant lady in all respects, who later went on to network. One morning, Renee was substitute host for the station's morning talk show. Her guests included the hearing impaired malaprop comic, Norm Crosby, and a woman doctor who was a sex advisor. Crosby did his segment and stuck around for the sex advice.

The advisor, let's call her Dr. Jean, was taking phone calls from people who, presumably, needed some sex advice. Eventually a caller named "Steve" was put through. "I'd like to direct this question to both Renee and Dr. Jean," Steve said meekly, in a voice that gave no indication of what was to come. "Um, I'm a little shy, but I'm wondering, uh, do either of you know where I could get a good fuck around here?"

The camera happened to be pointed at Renee at the moment the question was asked. She was smiling. Upon hearing the question, her expression changed not an iota, and she responded,

185

evenly, "Well, Steve, certainly not here. Good luck. We'll be back after this."

And she threw to a commercial break. The sex expert sat there in stunned silence, and Norm Crosby leaned over to Renee and asked, "Is it always like this around here?"

There had been no eight-second delay, and Steve's question and Renee's response went out over the airwaves. But Renee's coolness under fire, her refusal to react with shock or even change expression, and her perfect response meant viewers easily could have missed the exchange entirely, or doubted what they'd heard.

# As Long as You've Got Your Health

*The person who passed on this story swears it is true, even though it sounds like a variation of the old joke that ends, "What happened to the bagel slicer?" "They fired her, too."*

Back before videotape, news film was processed at the station. The film ran through several vats of chemicals. The temperature of these chemicals, usually around 100 degrees, was critical. Below that, the film would be underexposed; above it, it would be overexposed.

One day, the thermostat blew and the chemicals overheated. No one knew how to fix it or save the stock currently in the soup. The panicked head of the film lab ran to the news director's office for guidance. "We've got big problems," he said. "The film processor is up to 105 degrees. "Well," the news director responded, taking command of the situation, "if he's that sick, send him home."

# You Wouldn't Tease Me, Would You? Part 3

The same station, twice bitten by problems with the anchor, next tried a new approach to their news teases.

After the voice-over intoned words to the effect of, "Coming up on the news tonight, we'll have these fast-breaking developments," the director cut to the flashcam in the newsroom.

Viewers were then treated to fifteen seconds of silence and a picture of an empty chair.

# The Day the Reporter Busted Her Ass

Ice storm. The city paralyzed. Many reporters couldn't even make it in. One female reporter bravely got to the iced-over station parking lot. But as she walked in, her feet flew out from under her and she landed on the sidewalk squarely on her back. She was in agony.

It wasn't long before an employee discovered her and told the assignment desk to send for an ambulance. Because all ambulances were out on emergency calls, all that could be found was a fire truck.

Meanwhile, a rival station heard the words "fire truck" and the address on the emergency scanner and assumed the rival station was on fire. Their crew arrived about the same time as the fire truck, and the rivals got good footage of the injured competitor being carted off on a hook-and-ladder.

Because all the crews at her own station were out on assignment, no one got footage of their reporter down for the count. It took a bit of convincing, but they finally persuaded the rival station to give them a copy of the footage of their own injured reporter going to the hospital.

# Jim Beam Justice for the Late-Night News

It had been an unfortunate late show. A tape machine decided it did not like commercials. You just can't explain to a tape machine that commercials are the financial lifeblood of a television station. So at each commercial break, instead of running a thirty second spot at normal speed, as it was ordered to, the machine played them at twenty times normal speed. A half-minute ad flew by in three seconds with blurred video, and audio like a colony of chattering chipmunks.

I suspect many viewers would prefer it that way; however, sponsors do not. Once the techie brain trust realized what was happening, they had a choice between embarrassing the sponsor or embarrassing the anchors. The decision was easy.

So the break went something like this:

"We'll be back after this."

"*Screeple-dreeple-screeply-deep*" 20x audio and picture for three seconds. Five to ten seconds of black and dead air while techies try to solve problem. They don't, so . . .

Back to the studio, where one anchor is powdering her nose, the other telling a joke to the floor manager. The floor manager gets a terrified look, runs off-camera and signals the anchors to continue with the news. After a few seconds of confusion, one anchor says, "Are we back?" and begins shuffling through papers for some story to read, as the TelePrompTer is as blank as her expression.

"All right, in other news, police are searching for the killer of a nine-year-old . . . wait, we already did that story. We'll be right back after this message," she says, putting the ball back in the control room's court.

A three-second commercial break has been followed by a ten-second news segment. Then the process starts again.

This happened a few times with minor variations, as the playback continued to not air the commercials as God intended. By the end of the newscast, the anchors were almost proficient at surviving the micro-commercial/comedy break.

Unfortunately, due to the speeded-up commercials, the show was about five minutes short, which left the unfortunate anchors on the set trying to ad lib for five minutes.

The news director rarely stuck around for the 11 o'clock news but watched it at home. This took place after his cocktail hour, which this night apparently continued until the late news.

Unfortunately, he'd seen the newscast and was angry. Angry? Livid. He called the executive producer as the show ended and issued the following order: no one was allowed to leave the studio until after he was through talking with him. No one. No exceptions.

This had a number of unfortunate effects. For one thing, the techies, whose shift ended with the newscast, were now on golden time. For another, the innocent were netted with the guilty.

The ND started in with the show producer. The show producer had taken the call in the newsroom and most of the unfortunate prisoners gathered around to watch him spend more than a half hour listening to the news director's rant, occasionally holding the phone away from his ear or putting the receiver on the desk.

After midnight, a few of us decided to make a run for it. One guy had a baby sitter he had to take home. I just figured it was ludicrous; my piece had been okay, and he would never get around to me anyway. (He didn't, and the fact I left early was never mentioned. If it had, I'd have pleaded insanity.)

The ND ranted for another half hour or so, mostly to the unfortunate producer, before hanging up, freeing everyone to bolt.

Among those leaving an hour after the broadcast was a potential new hire who'd been invited to stick around and watch the news. He didn't take the job.

# Hard News Includes the Occasional *Steakout*

*This story was told to me and contains original writing by a reporter who prefers to remain anonymous.*

A rather new reporter was sent to cover the murder of a young woman. It seemed like a standard assignment at the time, but thanks in part to her coverage, the killer was caught. It's the kind of break every reporter wants. The victim's father even invited her to their home with a camera to interview him again so he could thank her.

Management loved the free positive publicity, and the young reporter was quite moved by the father's sincerity.

With the interview completed, the reporter returned to appear live on the set with the anchors. First there was a recap of her and the station's role in apprehending the killer.

Next she tossed to the videotape of the father thanking her and the station for helping end "the hell" he and his wife had gone through.

It was a momentous occasion in the career of the young reporter, the kind of expression of appreciation some never get in their lifetime. To add to the drama, the reporter herself had been deeply moved when she interviewed the parents, almost breaking down herself. She was considered by stationmates to be a class act, not a backstabbing, ambitious, claw-her-way-to-the-top type.

195

The tape ran, and throughout the city the sound of the father's voice could be heard, and even without seeing his face, you knew the words were sincere, the emotion heartfelt.

However . . .

Apparently, an engineer had forgotten to re-patch a cable from a machine that ran commercials in the break before the news. The machine retains a still frame from the last commercial it ran. In this case, the spot had been for a supermarket.

So while the father's *words* were heard, all the entire city got to see was a picture of a big, juicy, T-bone steak, with the words "Victim's Father" superimposed over it.

Inside the control room, there was shocked silence followed by the director repeating over and over again, "What the fuck is that?" and not saying "Take black" or "Go back to the studio" during the entire 20-second bite.

After the bite, the reporter, her grand moment turned into grand farce, managed to apologize for the mistake, before running off the set in shocked humiliation.

In the newsroom, everyone had stopped what he was working on and was paying rapt attention when the story began. Once they realized what had happened, they empathized in the traditional newsroom manner, by breaking into gut-wrenching peals of hysterical laughter.

The newsroom had barely recovered and sworn to each other not to make mention of the disaster as the reporter returned to the newsroom.

Of course, it took just one inevitable, uncontrollable snicker before everyone was in tears of laughter, except the reporter who was just in tears.

Also in the great tradition of newsrooms, they took her out and got her knee-walking drunk that night, and she went on to a long and successful career.

# TheYouthful-DemographicThat-AdvertisersCovet

## And Other Stuff You Can Learn from TV

# TheYouthfulDemographic-ThatAdvertisersCovet

You've heard it a thousand times, read it in the paper, too. It's gotten to the point that the phrase "the youthful demographic that advertisers covet" almost sounds like one, long, complex word that can stand by itself:

"Theyouthfuldemographicthatadvertiserscovet."

You read it on the entertainment pages, usually referring to a show being replaced or cancelled, or a newscast that's bringing in younger anchors, or another reality show being added to the mix. For those of you out of the loop, or whose loop itself has been mis-placed, here's what that means, literally and figuratively.

Theyouthfuldemographicthatadvertiserscovet literally refers to the young people with disposable income who tend to buy the products advertisers want to sell on TV.

Figuratively, it means, "Stand aside, you old fart. Kids bring in more money for us."

Can't argue with that. Too many geezers—and to advertisers geezerdom begins at about 35—many with disposable income, tend not to be good customers for advertising.

Example. I eat a certain brand of cereal for breakfast every morning. Oh, what the hell; they're not paying me, there's no con-flict of interest—it's Cheerios.

I'm not claiming it's the best cereal in the world, but it tastes just fine. I haven't eaten a cereal other than Cheerios in years. It's something I no longer have to think about. That's a good thing because I have too many other decisions to make each day in this multi-tasking, deregulated, compound-complex mess of a world.

Like what medicine to take. Used to be doctors decided what medicine worked for you. Now new prescription medicines run multi-page ads in magazines including six thousand words of fine print barely understood by doctors, much less patients. On TV, the ads shorten the fine print into a hasty, spoken "while this will cure your arthritis, and you should demand your doctor prescribe it now, you may get crushing headaches, projectile diarrhea, occasional heart stoppage, foul ooze flowing from your gums and total memory loss, and never again have an erection."

Ever since advertising for prescription medicines was legalized, the patient is expected to thumb through all this stuff and know what it means when the ad says, "In vitro studies indicate that celecoxib, although not a substrate, is an inhibitor of cytochrome P450 2D6." What all that fine print means is that if the stuff kills you, tough noogies, we warned you.

There's other time-consuming and complex decision-making thrust upon the consumer in these modern times. I now have to spend hours and days trying to find the lowest airfare, the correct phone service, the best cellular plan, drinkable wine and a car lease plan that doesn't cost me my mortgage. Business knows and takes advantage of the fact we are a nation of amateurs at most things in our lives, and they are the pros whose goal is to lead us—into their pocketbook.

Even once simple tasks like getting a non-prescription cough syrup are incredibly complicated. Once you just bought the cough syrup that tasted the worst, knowing that had to be the best for you.

Now, you must choose among different versions of the same brand. Do you want the syrup for "dry cough and dry heaves, but not fever," or the one for "a drippy snotlocker, hacking cough, congested uvula" or the one to soothe "chest cough, dry teeth and post nozzle drip"? There are a dozen mix-and-match combinations. And you can bet that after plunking down $11.95 for a "wheezy, slurpity, liquidy, shirt-soakity cough" syrup you'll walk outside and start a dry hack that sounds like a goat in a sandstorm.

So I've had to free up a lot of my time for these essential tasks, by putting aside my cereal decisions once and for all. If I see a clever, funny, or appealing ad on TV for Wheaties, I'll think, "There's a clever, funny, or appealing ad on TV for Wheaties," and the next day go out and buy more Cheerios.

That, in a nutshell, is why no one gives a rat's ass what Grandpa wants to watch on TV.

As a result, entertainment that might be enjoyed by geezers is replaced by entertainment aimed at people who still haven't made up their minds about what cereal to eat—or much else, for that matter. They're called: "Theyouthfuldemographicthatadvertiserscovet."

Well, it's free enterprise, right?

Try this sentence on for size. "The show, which appealed mostly to African-American audiences, was cancelled and replaced by a new show which appeals to that Caucasian demographic that advertisers covet."

Or: "No more Jews at eight. Our new program is aimed at that Christian demographic that advertisers covet."

That's discrimination, and it would be condemned by writers who use phrases like "Theyouthfuldemographicthatadvertiserscovet."

What irks me most is otherwise non-discriminatory good minds use such a phrase without thinking about what it really, truly means.

And so nobody lets out a peep while this form of age discrimination is celebrated every day.

And because news would rather sell products other than Depends, overage reporters and anchors and all are moved out so the young hotties—who also work cheaper—move in. That's good for the hotties who earn while they learn. When they learn what they need to know, often it's time for them to go because they no longer fit theyouthfuldemographicthatadvertiserscovet.

Now if you'll excuse me, my Cheerios are getting soggy.

# *American Beauty, Aunt Mary* and the Other Florida Vote

Here's something I'll bet you didn't know. Ninety-one percent of the viewers of a Palm Beach, Florida, TV station who answered a night-after-Oscar® survey did not think *American Beauty* deserved to win the Academy Award for Best Picture. The other nine percent went to Pat Buchanan.

I know you are sitting in amazement thinking, How does he come up with such vital and fascinating information? But hang on to your jodhpurs. This is of overwhelming significance. Okay, whelming significance, anyway.

I did not watch the Academy Awards in 2000. Not a minute of it. Not a second. There is an explanation. Like Best Picture winner *American Beauty*, it is a little complicated.

My favorite aunt, Aunt Mary, died. She slipped into a coma the day before the Academy Awards. I was her closest living relative and was on a plane from Los Angeles to Palm Beach the next morning.

While the unreal drama of the Oscars® went on in Beverly Hills, I was surrounded by real-life drama in the intensive care unit of Wellington Regional Medical Center. This once-vibrant, loving, tasteful and funny woman was hooked up to all manner of machines and breathing on a respirator. She wore no makeup; her blood pressure was critically low, propped up by the maximum dose of medication. She looked not at all as I'd known her.

The bad news came quickly. The doctor said there was very little chance she would survive the night, and I would have the responsibility of deciding whether to remove all "heroic," artificial measures of sustaining her life. Suddenly who won Best Sound Effects Editing didn't matter to me.

I spoke to her, prayed by her, held her hand. There was no indication whatsoever that she was aware of my presence. Around her, machines clicked and hummed, and bright red and green numbers flashed across screens. Her assisted respiration hovered at 12, her blood pressure was close to 65 over 30. Still, I could not make any decision other than to wait. Miracles happen.

I drove to the rented condo where Mary, widowed 23 years, had lived alone. By the time I arrived, there was an hour or so left of the awards and a television on which to view the show.

Instead, I searched for vital papers. Mary's condition had deteriorated so suddenly that she had made little preparation for her death, despite extremely poor health during the last two years.

An elegant and together woman in most situations, her organizational skills at home were not the best. But through fortune and her good planning I found the critical document I was searching for—her living will, signed in her own hand and properly witnessed. She requested that if she was in a terminal coma, she wished doctors to withdraw or withhold any and all extraordinary measures of sustaining life, except pain medication.

There were calls to be made the next morning to other relatives, friends and the acquaintances she made in 79 years on earth. But first I called the hospital. I learned Mary was not the least bit improved.

I drove there with the document in hand. Once at intensive care, I talked to the surgeon who had operated on her a few days before. "Irreversible coma" was one of the phrases he used. Zero chance of recovery. I handed over her living will, and a nurse photocopied it for their files. I was then handed a paper to initial. By the simple application of my initials, I granted her wish and requested on her behalf that they take no extraordinary measures to keep her alive, and shut down everything but pain medication.

Soon, Aunt Mary was gone.

It would take the better part of a week to go through the accumulations of a life of almost eight decades. More papers to sign, even more to throw out or turn over to the estate. There were lawyers and priests and undertakers and phone calls to relatives and friends. At bedtime, I'd flop into one of her sofas and turn on the TV and watch what news was like in Palm Beach.

Palm Beach, until it found infamy in the 2000 presidential brouhaha, was known as the land where old, wealthy New Yorkers go to die. Parts of its downtown could double for Beverly Hills, except the palm trees have coconuts, the ocean is closer and the guys with neck chains are retirees, not producers. Palm Beach is on the east coast of Florida, about an hour or so up the 95 from Miami.

In fact, the "Palm Beaches" extend up and down the coast, on the thin strip of land that forms the eastern edge of the inter-coastal waterway. West Palm Beach, logically, is west of the area, and just south of it is Lantana, the home of *The National Enquirer*.

To the north is Jupiter, where Burt Reynolds used to have his dinner theater. A small town called Hypoluxo, near South Palm Beach, is home to restaurants where you can sit at the bar and watch waiters hand drinks over a railing to customers on an eighty-foot cabin cruiser pulled up to the dock. Mansions dominate the area just south of Palm Beach, down the coast. As you get farther south, there are large condos owned and sometimes occupied mostly by "snowbirds," Northerners with money enough for a second home and a dislike of Northern winters.

On the radio, a number of stations feature formats you could call "Music for God's waiting room." The area skews really old, as the boys in advertising like to say. The beautiful beaches seem uncrowded, and the lifeguard stations shut down at 5 P.M.

At one point, I saw a sign reading "Caution! Ocean Shore Rocks!" In Palm Beach, that serves as a warning; in Fort Lauderdale, the same sign could be a suggestion that if you're not ready to party hearty, take your act elsewhere.

Back to our movie survey. It is unlikely the liberal elderly of the Palm Beaches were inclined to vote favorably for *American Beauty*—or that they were even up late enough to participate in the survey. One suspects that most of those polled were taken from the ranks of stereotypical Southerners who also call Palm

Beach home. Many of them, obviously, do not have the same tastes as those who make movies like *American Beauty*. Most likely it was they who made up the nine out of ten who did not favor *American Beauty* for the Oscar.®

There are other indications the area is not as sophisticated as one might think. I heard a radio station advertise a traveling company of *The Phantom of the Opera* that featured "*Welcome Back Kotter*'s Ron Palillo as the Phantom." I'm almost certain they were serious.

While on the road, you must keep constantly alert for seemingly driverless Cadillacs going twenty with the left blinker on. They mix easily with pickups with a Rebel flag in the window and a dog in the back. Some clichés are true.

Without putting too fine a point on it, I suspect the average Floridian can't identify with a movie about a mid-life-crisis–suffering, pot-smoking, job-quitting, cheerleader-lusting, talking dead guy, who narrates and stars in a movie about how he got to be dead because of his cheating, obsessive, careerist chatterbox wife; his uncommunicative, messed-up, in-love daughter; her lusty, virgin, upwardly-mobile cheerleader friend; her drug-selling, abused, video-obsessive boyfriend; and his repressed, gay Marine colonel, paranoid and abusive father.

Hollywood refers to everything between New York City and LaLa Land as "the Land We Fly Over." And balancing the art that appeals to more sophisticated audiences and more populist entertainment is one reason movie making is such a difficult task. Because it is so much easier and profitable to aim at the unsophisticates and those who live in the Land We Fly Over, most of the time that's the way Hollywood does it. And for those of us who review or reviewed movies, it's a hard lesson to learn.

# Send Richard Hatch
# to the Moon

During the hysteria surrounding the big breakthrough in reality television of the new millennium, a CBS publicist said of one new CBS television show:

> I can't think of a comparable level of cultural excitement about something since Neil Armstrong landed on the moon in the 1960s.

The CBS hypester was speaking of the television program *Survivor.*

Honest.

Really. He said that.

Maybe he was drunk.

Otherwise, one must ask, has the former Tiffany network convinced itself that the moon landing, one of the crowning achievements of humankind, should be mentioned in the same breath with that appalling soap opera?

Even allowing for marketing hyperbole, I ask: Who is this boob? Was he *even* *alive* when Neil Armstrong landed on the moon? Probably not. I was. I watched it. I watched Cronkite cry through my own teary eyes. A space program, goaded by an overseas threat, had literally risen from the ashes of booster rockets exploding on the launch pad and achieved what a slain president had promised years before.

And when mankind leaped those surly bounds of earth and landed on another heavenly object for the first time ever, the effect was nothing like the "cultural excitement" caused by an islandful of losers stabbing one another in the back while surrounded by technical equipment.

Landing on the moon was an amazing accomplishment that involved more than the two men who walked there and the one who waited in orbit. Thousands of people had spent millions of hours to make sure a zillion lowest bidder–provided parts worked for the best-of-the-best human beings whose lives depended on them.

I was reminded of the accomplishment by a Discovery Channel documentary about the explosion of the Challenger and death of the astronauts and the teacher aboard it.

The program reported that the technicians at Morton Thiokol, who helped build the solid-fuel rocket that caused the explosion, unanimously recommended a launch "no-go" because the temperature on the launch pad dropped below freezing, well under the recommended no-go level. These scientists believed the astronauts were in grave danger because rubberized "O-rings" on the solid rocket boosters were not designed for those temperatures.

The engineers were overruled by four managers who gave the "go" and said the seals would hold. The engineers couldn't even watch the launch, convinced as they were that the rocket and the spacecraft would blow up on the launch pad.

It is a truth that no matter how demeaning television reality shows get—*Big Brother* and *Temptation Island* lead the pack as this is written—there are some things that give a viewer hope. Discovery has consistently presented informative and well-made documentaries that are more gripping than the pathetic machinations of the greedheads who clutter the tube's reality fare today.

The Challenger disaster, the moon landing, the space program itself involved real heroes acting for the greater good.

Compare that with the goofballs selected primarily for their demographic appeal, the conniving, selfish, scheming, grub-eating geeks who—spurned on by the thought of wealth—did whatever they could get away with to assure that they would get their million-buck bounty. Plus a Pontiac Aztek. (No truth to the rumor that second prize was *two* Pontiac Azteks.)

Of the top original *Survivor* finalists, one was under criminal investigation for alleged child abuse (the charges were later dropped). Another faced an outstanding arrest warrant for alleged credit card theft. A third told a fellow survivor that she wouldn't pee on her if she were on fire.

And what ever happened to them? In case anyone cares, the original *Survivor* gang may now be found sipping margaritas with Darva Conger and Kathie Lee Gifford at the Been Good To Know Ya Ex-Celebrity Cafe.

And this first batch was apparently only a warm-up. As this is written, I haven't seen anything but the promos for *Survivor II*, but this crew is being portrayed as even more conniving, devious, sexier and hotter than the first group.

And they'll have to go some to match the orgy of on- and off-camera carnality that is the goal of *Temptation Island*, a reprehensible program, even by Fox standards.

I know a lot of it is just marketing, but *really*.

Well, it could have been worse. Imagine if *Survivor* producers had been running the space program. They'd probably have insisted that before returning home, the moon astronauts vote one of their members off the spacecraft.

# The Agony and the Slam Dunkery

I caught one of those NBA triple-headers on NBC. I was well entertained by the various NBC broadcast teams, Ahmad, Doug, the Big Redhead and Mr. Lingerie, among others. (Actually the NBA isn't the NBA without Marv Albert, and I'm glad he's back after serving his time in celebrity jail.) *Yeeesssssssss!!!!!!*

Celebrity jail, incidentally, is that place disgraced celebs go for a period of time between the shocking or disturbing news that puts them there and the time when the public and potential employers forgive and forget.

I'm happy the network has now returned Albert to visibility, even if they made the decision because his extreme talent and popularity help them make money. The NBA needs more money, and has since Jordan retired. And they've lost fans because of the growing realization that regular season NBA basketball is mostly just an exhibition until crunch time. And, of course, many players are spoiled and overpaid. So more fans realize it would be better to use money earmarked for two courtside seats and instead put a down payment on a car.

Now NBC has gone to great effort to increase at-home excitement by bringing the game of basketball even closer to viewers. One way is by putting microphones everywhere they can—on the ref, on the sidelines, under the basket. For a while they wanted mikes in the huddle, but paranoid coaches (forgive the redundancy) and inarticulate players (ditto) said no, absolutely not.

211

So let's talk about the mikes under the basket. If you were to listen only to those mikes you would think you were watching a tickle fight at a girls' pajama party combined with a Medieval torture chamber. I haven't heard so many shrieks of agony since Richard Simmons got his legs waxed on *The View*.

Hey, don't get me wrong. I have great admiration for athletes, particularly large, muscled ones who can hurt me. Many popular sports demand not only skill but also the kind of courage that never admits to pain:

**Boxing:** Guys with faces looking like a dropped bottle of ketchup bob up from repeated knockdowns, keep coming back for more punishment and beg the ref not to stop the fight. Despite brutal beatings, not a peep of pain.

**Baseball:** You get hit by a ninety-mile heater and *you are not allowed to rub*. This may be why so many batters charge the mound after getting plunked. In the ensuing scrum they can rub where it hurts while no one's looking. But there is no denying that baseball players are proud and brave and don't let an opponent know they hurt them. Not a peep of pain.

**Football:** Bone-crunching action as a matter of course. Break a bone? Wrap it in gauze and get back out there. Three-hundred–pound men colliding at fierce speeds. Crack backs. Cut blocks. Smashmouth. Perhaps the most brutal of team sports. Yet, time and again they will drag themselves back out for more. Not a peep of pain.

**Hockey:** Nightly assault and battery on skates. Fights break out every night. Take a puck in the piehole? You have the trainer throw 65 stitches into it, and take your next shift. Not a peep of pain.

Then there's basketball, where seven-foot, 300 pounders with bodies by Zeus and guns like howitzers scream like little girls every time someone gets near them.

*AYIIIIIIIIIIIIIEEEEEEEEEEEEEEEEEE!!!!!!* It's a 280-pound power forward, the victim of a positioning nudge no harder than what old ladies get each day on the subway.

*ARRRRRRRGGGGGGGGGGGHHHHHHHHHHHHHHHH!!!* Someone has just tried to post up and boompsie-daisied a 290-pound center with arms like tree trunks. He screams like he's been tazered in the genitals.

*OOOOOOOOOWWWWWWWWWWWWWWWWW!!!!*
shouts a chiseled and cut picture of muscles as a light breeze wafts
in from an arena door as he goes up for a rebound.

In addition to the screams, many of these behemoths fall like
redwoods when someone goes 'round their pick. Others snap
backward as if hit by a load of buckshot at the touch of an opponent brushing past them.

Oh, the humanity.

The only places you'll hear greater cries of anguish are at an
Iraqi welcome wagon in Kurdistan or on a soccer field. No professional soccer match is complete without some guy getting his
tootsie stepped on, falling to the turf clutching his shin in agony,
and wailing so loud he can be heard over the hooligans killing one
another in the stands.

The stretcher is brought out, the corpse of the injured player
removed. The ref finally produces a yellow card and *then* the dead
guy jumps up and trots back into play without a limp.

Basketball fans know the real reason for all the screaming in
the night. It's just bad actors trying to convince the ref they've been
mortally wounded and should have a deuce from the line before
they bleed to death. It's more fake than the WWF. The refs know
it, the players know it, the fans know it, and the play-by-play guys
ignore it.

And, yeah, basketball is no game for sissies. There are major
collision and thudding fouls under the basket. Those usually pro-
duce—silence.

I think the histrionics and shouts of pain will soon be incorporated into the excitement. I think any time a player howls in agony
he should either (a) be awarded an additional free throw for a convincing performance or (b) lose a free throw for being a ham actor.

Or at the very least, the local sports guy should put a few of
these cries together and see if he can't come up with a novelty
record, kind of like those barking, Christmas-caroling dogs.

# Trying on Briefs

*TV has generously allowed feminine hygiene and incontinence products to grace the tube. But what about ambulance chasers?*

I saw a letter in *ShopTalk* recently defending the rights of contingency lawyers to advertise during newscasts. The writer spoke rousingly in support of those barristers who make their services available to victims of aviation disasters.

Let me add my own kind words about the dedicated contrail chasers who selflessly abandon their snuggle beds to hustle themselves to crash sites, the better to ensure that the death of a loved one shouldn't be a total loss for the victim's next-of-kin.

As my former personal mouthpiece, the extinguished G. Beelzebub Wellington, Esq., once so aptly put it: "Thank God for contingency fees. It saves a helluva lot of phonied-up paperwork." He added that to assure timely arrival at crash sites, many contingency lawyers have been forced, at considerable personal expense, to upgrade their personal transport to more powerful Vipers and Turbo-Beemers.

The author of the letter notes quite accurately that lawyers are not permitted to solicit business one-on-one at crash sites. In that respect, one might compare them to hookers in a barroom, allowed to be there as long as they don't admit their purpose or ask naive gin-swillers if they want a date.

I guess my question is this, although with me it's always hard to tell: Just who the hell came up with that 33 percent contingency fee gold mine anyway? Agents get ten percent or less, managers 15 percent. The only people who get more than lawyers are the IRS, Don King and California wives—at least until they pay *their* lawyers.

I agree that even the seediest misery-chasers have the right to share the airwaves with the penile implanters, garden suppliers and romantic forecasters who also inhabit the world of advertising. I would never deny a lawyer the same rights offered hose fixers, hose sellers and hokey psychics.

To me, nothing shouts "free enterprise" more than switching over to Country Music Television for a late-night country-music fix and instead finding some lard-butt Master Psychic listening to a mono-browed philanderer gush, "However did you know I was having an affair with my husband's duck?"

And nothing gets my First Amendment juices flowing faster than seeing some ethics-challenged bonehead with pockmarks bigger than his moral compass inviting felons to dial 1-900-SHYSTER "if you tripped over a kiddie toy while fleeing from the house you just burglarized."

Now, don't get your panties in a bunch, counselors, or worse yet, sue me for definition of character. It's just good old-fashioned Constitutionally-guaranteed satire. I know the contingency fee is a necessary evil. And, knowing you're out there raises the oft-battered self-esteem of those professional mike-jockeys in TV who have to ask grieving widows, "What's it like to know your beloved husband will never come through your door again?"

# Academy Award Season and Other Conspiracies

As a conspiracy theorist of the first water, I've watched certain recent developments with close attention and increased alarm. These events took place around the time of the Academy Awards in the spring of 2001:

- Jennifer Lopez arrived at the Academy Awards with her hootenannies in plain view.
- Matt Drudge claimed that Tim Russert will replace CBS anchor Dan Rather, citing highly-placed sources within the conservative media propaganda apparatus eager to denigrate perceived liberals.
- Bozo the Clown was fired.
- Julia Roberts forgot to thank Erin Brockovich during her long, rambling acceptance speech for winning the Oscar® for playing Erin Brockovich in the movie *Erin Brockovich*.
- Ratings of the Oscar® broadcast slipped.
- Ratings of XFL football on NBC plummeted to *My Mother the Car* levels. (This despite the fact that *My Mother the Car* is currently not on the air.)
- Feud broke out between a Los Angeles TV broadcaster and a *Los Angeles Times* TV critic.

Seemingly unrelated events? Your mother's mustache. By using sourcing methodology currently accepted by what passes for the media these days, and by using accepted methodology of TV psychics with 900 numbers, I can firmly state, without fear of contraception, that the following will take place within the coming year or so:

- Jennifer Lopez will anchor *The CBS Nightly News*. Weekends will be hosted by her caboose.
- Bozo the Clown will be appointed new chairman of the Fed.
- Oscars® will be canceled because of low ratings, just like the XFL.
- Erin Brockovich will star in new Fox series *My Mother the Car* with the catchphrase "Wait'll You Get a Load of *These* Headlights." She will win an Emmy, forget to thank Julia Roberts.
- Tim Russert and Dan Rather will announce their engagement.

Actually, that's nonsense. Maybe one of those predictions will come true. But that should be more than enough for me to become an overrated gossip guru. I could make millions spreading political propaganda under the guise of news, and then watch it blossom into full-fledged self-fulfilling prophecies to be spread by other media too lazy to check the facts themselves. Hey, not the classiest job on the planet, but it's a living.

As usual, the 2001 Academy Award pre- and post-game shows were at least as much fun to watch as the show itself. My favorite pre-show moment came from a local TV entertainment person doing live coverage of arrivals, who said, "The oddest fashion accessory I've seen is there's some guy, who apparently is in the band, has his guitar on his back." At that point, the guy, whose name is Yo-Yo Ma, came over with his cello case on his back to exchange pleasantries.

I've been there. I've worked the line and it's hot and sweaty and crowded and noisy and overfilled with celebrity gridlock. Your questions are vapid and silly because there's little time to ask anything more significant than "How are you feeling?" "Are you nervous?" or "Who designed the dress you're almost wearing, Ms. Lopez?"

Fox's local post-show coverage was highlighted by someone named Jillian, to whom a speed freak might reasonably suggest, "For God's sake, lady, calm down!" Jillian was under the impression the Academy Awards were merely a backdrop to her own one-woman show.

Instead of turning the whole shebang over to the after-show parties, Fox News Eleven chose to run its ten o'clock news, interrupted by live Oscar® party coverage every few minutes. It was a little jarring to go from Jillian shouting, "I'm so vain, you probably think this night is about you," back to the studio and an anchor intoning, "We'll be back with more party coverage, but first, three people were killed today as . . ."

As for the feud between *Los Angeles Times* TV critic Howard Rosenberg and TV entertainment reporter Sam Rubin, as of this writing it's like most media feuds: no casualties, and self-promotion for all.

It started when Rosenberg ripped Rubin for being, among other things, "a pillow with lips." Sam wrote back to mock Rosenberg's work schedule and challenge him to switch jobs for a week.

As much as I enjoyed seeing my good showbiz friend and former colleague Sam get up on his hind legs and fight back against the slings and arrows of Rosenberg, I'm afraid Sam is straying into dangerous ground.

Sam sets up a dangerous precedent by claiming Howard should walk a mile in TV Boy's Guccis before he is qualified to take a potshot at him. Sam notes: "It's one thing to write about it; it's another thing to actually try to pull it off."

See, the trouble there is that any actor Sam has criticized over the years could well take the same attitude. What right does a holly-jolly TV reviewer have to claim to understand the nuances of acting, without trying to act himself? And not just by doing the occasional freeloader cameos critics are asked to do; I'm talking about a genuine acting gig. "If you can't do, review" is an ugly can of worms no critic wants opened.

The other problem is that Sam claims the entire nation is full of morning news and yak shows inspired by his KTLA version, hence his show is more admirable than Rosenberg's less-emulated *L.A. Times* Calendar section. The only fly in Sam's imitation-is-flattery ointment is that the most emulated national

TV shows are *Survivor* and *Jackass*. Does popularity equal quality?

I guess what I'm trying to say is, I wish these two kids would kiss and make up. Well, make up anyway. If the job switch takes place, I volunteer to be on the judging panel. I'd like to see justice served, and I could use a taste of the free self-promotional publicity show-biz feuds stir up.

# So, What's the Deal with Jim Lehrer?

*This was written shortly after the first presidential debate, and updated in February 2001.*

The governor of the Great State of California has vetoed a bill that would allow journalists to interview guests of the California penal system. The Reporters Committee for Freedom of the Press, which is an even more impressive-sounding title than "Governor of the Great State of California," immediately condemned his decision. I'm not sure whether I agree or disagree, but by God, it's nice to have an organization of feisty journalists give 'em the old what-for.

Yet when Fox and NBC decided not to carry the Bush/Gore debates live, and instead carry baseball or regular programming, the mighty voice of the Radio-Television News Directors Association was silent. The RTNDA refused to condemn Fox or NBC for brazenly choosing naked commerce over showing the American people the first promising cure for insomnia in decades.

By 2004, when almost all network TV shows will be spin-offs of *Survivor*, the presidential debates must be a little livelier or they'll never get on the air.

I mean, was that debate dull, or what? And speaking of dull, what the heck's the deal with Jim Lehrer?

There were more fat pitches lobbed up than at a whole season of seniors' slow-pitch softball. Was it me, or did every question begin, "Mr. (Vice President/Governor), would you mind giving us your stump speech on (Medicare/Education/Social Security)?"

Lehrer pointed out before the debate that he alone thought up all his questions. He should have hired Bruce Vilanch. There was even breaking news Lehrer ignored. The *Los Angeles Times* had reported that very day that hundreds of jailbirds, druggies and Alzheimer's victims with Bush-approved carry permits and .357 Magnums in their pants have been shooting innocent citizens throughout Texas. Sure, the story all but disappeared in the next few days, but it was big news that night. Would it kill Lehrer to ask about it?

Jim Lehrer is an oft-honored, highly respected and brilliant newsman that millions, myself included, admire greatly as a giant of journalism. Of all the news programs I hardly ever watch, his is by far my favorite. In sports terminology, I am the first to admit I couldn't carry his jock. Not that I'd want to carry his jock. In fact, I don't think journalists have jocks, or people to carry one for them. I do know that on Chris Matthews's *Hardball*, guests are issued complimentary protective cups.

Where was I? Oh, Jim Lehrer. I love the guy, which is why his performance at the debates was disappointing. Not that Tweedles Dumb and Dee were much help, but I've seen better questions on *The Family Feud*. He's the wrong man for the wrong show. You don't need to be the sharpest bulb in the shoebox to know he needs to be replaced for the next debate, if only because he brings too much dignity to the proceedings. And it's not as if there aren't better people for the job.

The list includes Bill Maher, Oprah, Little Dickie Dawson, Mean Gene Okerlund, Tom Bergeron, Stuttering John, Jeff Probst, Monte Hall (if he's still alive), Dennis Miller, Conan O'Brian, Don Imus—in fact, anybody with a pulse and an attitude. Get someone like Dan Ackroyd to ask: "(George/Al), you ignorant slut, what are your thoughts on abortion?" Find someone who will break through the rehearsed, focus-grouped, research-enhanced veneer slathered over these guys like Katherine Harris's makeup. Okay, it's too late for this presidential term, but it's not too early to plan for 2004.

While we're on the topic, will someone puh-LEESE stop the parade of beleaguered "typical" Americans who were dragged out of their homes and spirited off to Boston with their Winnebagoes and their poodles to stand as mute (and unseen) testimony to the Innate Goodness of whichever candidate happened to find them first?

Fresh ideas are desperately needed. I call upon the mighty intellectuals of America to come up with new ways to enliven the debates and move them beyond lockboxed Medicare and fuzzy math.

Perhaps, they could introduce a counting device to indicate each time Dubya proves English is his second language, or Gore gets that goofy expression on his grill and looks like my Uncle Ned when he's swacked on Jamaican Overproof. Maybe they could steal Letterman's plan to have Don Rickles come by to "drop his pants and fire a rocket."

Do something, anything. Don't make me watch *Survivor* instead.

# Some Thoughts on the Post-Election Crisis

*During the three days following the non-election of 2000, I sat down and wrote a series of one-liners about the event.*

## November 8

- Network executives are rushing moist towelettes to network anchors to wipe the egg off their faces. The anchors said they were thankful for the towelettes, no wait, they weren't thankful, hold it a sec, well, now it's too close to call if they're thankful.
- In Florida, a vote for Nader was actually a vote for Bush, and a vote for Gore was apparently a vote for Buchanan.
- Seeking to relax under the enormous stress, George Bush watched videos of recent Texas executions, and Al Gore played his own stump speeches to help catch some much-needed shuteye.
- Today, *USA Today* said it will have yesterday's results tomorrow.
- Missouri Republican senatorial candidate John Ashcroft, who lost to a dead guy, announced he will run for the AFL-CIO presidency next year against Jimmy Hoffa.
- CBS brass vetoed new promotional spots that said, "Hey, no matter who eventually wins, we got it wrong first!"
- Darva Conger called a press conference this morning to declare she would have no comment on the election and would the media please, for the love of God, just leave her alone. She also

announced her engagement to Richard Hatch and an upcoming nude spread in *Popular Mechanics*.

# November 9

- A confused former president George Bush has just conceded the election to Iraqi strongman Saddam Hussein.
- A Fox News Channel spokesman said a software glitch in a computer used for both election results and BCS standings is to blame for the network's announcement last night that "the next president of the United States is the Nebraska Cornhuskers."
- A ruling by the Supreme Court has extended the deadline for absentee ballots from swamp-dwelling UFO-abducted Floridians by a week.
- Darva Conger called another press conference this afternoon to announce that if Bush wins, she will adopt Elian Gonzalez and marry the Mormon Tabernacle Choir.
- The Florida Election Board has reversed an earlier decision to allow husbands and wives who are also brother and sister to vote twice each.
- Pat Buchanan, disappointed with his showing, has gone into seclusion either in Argentina or by signing on for a new UPN sitcom.

# November 10

- An embittered Joe Lieberman cussed out elderly Jews today for being confused, then locked himself into his hotel room with a new director's-cut DVD of *Debbie Does Dallas*.
- Dick Cheney, looking chagrined and still bald, told pool reporters "If I'd known elections could be this close, I might have registered to vote years ago."
- Meanwhile, vice president maybe elect, maybe not elect Dick Cheney's wife, maybe second lady elect Lynn Cheney, told pool reporters to get the hell out of their pool.
- Dan Rather publicly apologized to his CBS viewing audience last night, claiming his "mind frequency" had been taken over on election night by the spirit of the late "Tennessee" Ernie Ford.

- An obviously upset Chris Matthews today ordered himself to "shut the hell up and stop interrupting people" and then pantsed Cokie Roberts.
- It may just be a coincidence, but White House sources report that Bill Clinton has ordered new draperies for the Oval Office and a fresh batch of interns for himself.
- A pale and haggard Walter Mondale called a press conference this morning to ask reporters whether he "still has a shot."

# New Mottos

- **Fox News:** "We're New at This. Usually It Takes Years to Screw Up This Bad."
- **MSNBC:** "Hey, We Were Wrong, but Our Anchor Is Cuter Than Yours."
- **ABC News**: "What Did You Expect? We're Owned by Disney. You Know, Inventor of Fantasyland. Duh!"
- **UPN:** "The Only Network That Didn't Get It Wrong!"
- **CBS News:** "We're Sorry as a Coonskin Cap Hangin' from the Backside of a Southbound Mule in the Rain."
- **CNN:** "Our Jeff Greenfield Is Smarter Than Anyone Else Who Got It Wrong."
- **WB:** "Are We Still on the Air?"
- **Nostalgia Network:** "Dewey Defeats Truman."

# The Best Sports Department Ever

I watched the final *Sports Night* with a tear in my eye. The show was canceled to make room for more Greed TV—specifically, a fourth night of *Who Wants to Be a Millionaire?* A contributing factor was neglect.

I loved the first season of the show. It was original, hilarious, marvelously acted, insider-true, unpredictable, and filled with emotion and extraordinary dialogue.

Well, okay, maybe not exactly insider-true. No one in the real world is that smart, that loving, that dependable, that intrinsically good. But we all like to think of ourselves as such.

*Sports Night* was created and written by Aaron Sorkin, who wrote most of the episodes himself in his unique and brilliant style and then a year later sold his soul to the White House.

The second season of *Sports Night* took a back seat to Sorkin's new project *The West Wing*, which also happens to be brilliant. Unlike *Sports Night*, it has proved a ratings as well as critical success.

Sorkin wrote many if not most of *The West Wing*'s episodes, too. The playwright/screenwriter who wrote two wonderful films—*The American President* and *A Few Good Men*—brought his full creative powers to bear on *The West Wing*, which suffered from remarkably few missteps.

But such artistry comes with a cost. Sorkin has battled substance abuse problems. And another sufferer was *Sports Night*.

The show lost its way in its sophomore season and never had a chance, despite one of the best ensembles in television and sporadically brilliant episodes.

*Sports Night* was a show that needed constant care and nurturing. Its strength was its delicacy—the long flowing shots, the perfect rhythms of its screwball-comedy–style dialogue, its handling of work and personal relationships, its occasional character speeches that conveyed moral lessons at times as well as the master, Frank Capra.

With Sorkin's care and attention diverted, the show lost focus. Storylines came and went, as did the show itself on ABC. Regular viewership habits never had a chance to develop.

Then again, the show took a terrible hit with the temporary loss and reduced appearances of Robert Guillaume as the *paterfamilias* to the kids.

Hey, wait, isn't that the guy who played *Benson?* No, man, that's an actor. Should have seen him in *The Phantom of the Opera*. In *Sports Night* he was invaluable, a wise and understanding perfect boss type, who attracted extraordinary workers to what was described as a third-rate and third-rated sports network.

If the characterizations sound familiar, Sorkin used the same formula with *The West Wing*. Much as that show would not be the same without Martin Sheen's portrayal of the wise and understanding perfect boss type who attracted extraordinary workers to the White House, so too was *Sports Night* seriously harmed by Guillaume's serious stroke.

You can't blame Sorkin for *Sports Night*'s demise. As actors and directors of *The West Wing* have pointed out when accepting Emmy and Golden Globe honors, every week Sorkin presents them with a perfect little 45-minute movie. Such writing comes with extreme effort, and there are only so many hours in the day.

*Sports Night* finished its two-year run with optimism. The fate of the show was up in the air when the final episode was shot; there were rumors it might be revived on a cable net. (Reruns have been seen on the Comedy Channel, but no new episodes were shot.)

The blind optimism of the characters on-screen, who so wanted to keep their magical TV land together, was certainly called for.

On the show, the fictional CSC network had been purchased and saved. The last scenes we saw were of the jubilant cast of the fictional show ecstatic that life would go on. It's a way I'd like to remember them, fighting the good fight to the very end, choosing quality over cheap ratings ploys, doing and saying what's right no matter the consequences, falling in and out of love with one another.

When it was cooking, *Sports Night* conveyed part of the addiction that television news (or sports) has to its practitioners. The pure adrenaline rush, the joyful chaos that sometimes leads to art, the relationships, the wit, the insanity, the kind of bonding not often found outside locker rooms and foxholes, makes up for a lot of the agonies.

Timing is everything. The show was just warming up, and its premature death deprived all of us of marvelous seasons to come.

# I Hate My Cable Company

I hate my cable company. I hated the old cable company and now it's been bought by a new company and I hate them, too. Why? Because as soon as they took over they jacked up rates. Cable uses any excuse to jack up rates. Full moon? Jack up rates. New fall season? Jack up rates. Need fresh potpourri for the conference room? Jack up rates.

Once my cable company said they had to jack up rates because their president was "feeling a little blue."

Here's my new fee schedule, which has undoubtedly been jacked up again since this was written:

- Basic Cable Fee — $21.95
- Linkage Costs — $9.95
- Basic Satellite Package — $9.50
- Super Satellite Package — $10.00
- Missing Satellite Package — $3.50
- Crashed Satellite Cleanup and Disposal Package — $2.50
- Booze and Hookers for Lobbyists — $2.50
- Digital Phrelman — $9.95
- Phrelman Converter Box — $2.50
- A Taste for Mrs. Phrelman — $1.50
- Special Fee to Prevent Ron Popeil from Ever Dropping By — $3.50
- Sequins for Richard Simmons — $1.50

- Annual Undercharge Overage Fee                              $10.00
- Connection Charge                                            $1.00
- Reconnection Charge                                          $1.00
- Erection Charge                                              $5.00
- Fed Gov't Excise Tax                                         $1.50
- Fed Gov't Exercise Tax                                       $1.50
- Biscuits for Lassie                                            N/C
- New Pants for Cable Guy That Won't Show
  His Butt-Crack                                               $2.50

I'm paying for some 80 stations, most of which run nothing but an English guy with Pickup Sticks teeth telling a dim blond woman how to cook an omelet on his "amazing new cookware."

To add to the jack-up, the gang at Cable Central, with nothing else to do, just played "move the stations." As victim of occupationally induced Newsheimers Disease and possessed of rapidly dissipating short-term memory, it took me about a year to memorize the numbers for all the old stations. Now for my extra monthly fee, I get to play "Where the hell's MSNBC?" on my remote. Along the way, I think they deleted the Fox AntiChrist Network, and all I get on the Disney Channel now is Michael Eisner telling me to send him all the money I have, no questions asked.

The Weather Channel used to be Channel 43. Now it's Channel 12. Nobody watches the Weather Channel in L.A. because there is no weather in L.A. Any time a seagull sneezes, local stations pre-empt everything but car chases to go on Storm Watch until the storm leaves or their weathercaster's pompadour collapses. In L.A., weathermen have prettier locks than a televangelist with a Rogaine fetish. You can check surf conditions by watching the break on KABC's Dallas Raines' hair. Yeah, that's his name. They've got a guy named Johnny Mountain, too.

Regarding the jacked-up rates, I did what I always do when my cable company raises rates. I called to complain. After several duels with their automated answering service, I got a recorded message from Tom Brokaw threatening that if I didn't stop whining he'd write another book.

One week later, I received a brochure describing the new channels my new cable company had added.

**The Boils and Cysts Network.** 24 hours a day of doctors lancing boils and removing cysts. Highlights: the annual "Skin Tag and Wartathon," a sports show called *Bowling for Cysts*, and *Boil-Lancing Self Taught* with Geena Davis. Daily health segments include Melanoma Monday, "It's Not a Tumor" Tuesday (hosted by Arnold Schwarzenegger), Warty Wednesday, Tubercle Thursday and Festering Furunculus Friday.

**The Miniature Golf Channel.** (Formerly "Putt-Putt.") Miniature golf from around the world. Highlights include their award-winning miniseries *Windmill Holes of Holland*. New programming includes *Extreme Putt-Putt*, in which opponents check each other into the weeds during play. Jesse Ventura and Tiger Woods host.

**The All Fat Guy Network.** As the name implies, nothing but fat guys 24/7. *Fat Guy Road Trip*, *Watching Fat Guys Eat*, *Who Wants to Marry a Fat Guy?* (hosted by John Goodman), *Good Eats for Fat Guys*, and featuring the famous Heimlich Honeys, the only cheerleading squad that averages a quarter ton per cheerleader.

**Cage Match Court Channel.** Hosted by Mean Gene Okerlund. Just like regular court shows, except plaintiff and defendant are put in a locked cage for a no-holds-barred, loser-leaves-town Texas death match.

**Worst of Fox Network.** Highlights of car crashes, animal attacks, and Fox reality series already carried on one of the 35 other Fox channels. Also, an original reality series chronicling the lives of a houseful of proctologists, called *Rectum? Damn Near Killed 'Em*.

**The Geezer Channel.** Best known for their new reality series *Senility Island*, in which a dozen old folks are sent to play shuffleboard and reminisce. Each week, one is voted off the island and euthanized.

# How to Stop Violence in Media? Study It to Death

Their mama won't let them grow up to be cowboys, and I've warned them of the dangers of following Pop into the media, but now I know what I want my kids to be.

Ribbon salesmen. Specifically, blue ribbon salesmen. There will never be a shortage of need for blue ribbons. There's the long-standing steady base of orders from county fairs and dog shows, but where it's become a real growth industry is in the world of blue ribbon commissions.

Never in the history of civilization have there been so many blue ribbon commissions studying really important stuff. (Actually I just made that up. On the spot. And utterly without conscience. I've recently appointed a blue ribbon commission to investigate my tendency to draw my conclusions in crayon.)

Blue ribbon commissions are usually formed when immediate action is needed to counter a crisis, but no one wants to take the bull by the tail and face the situation. Blue ribbon commissioners figure if they set everybody to studying an issue long enough, there's time to lie low until everybody moves on to the next crisis and forgets about the current one.

Blue ribbon commissions are announced with great fanfare and bombast. They consist of retired geniuses, a representative of the business community, a member of the clergy or two, and, to enhance the pizzazz factor, someone who once dated Madonna.

The commission disappears for three years of hearings and study, then announces findings that nobody reads except the person charged with forming a new blue ribbon commission to study the results of the original one.

The latest blue ribbon commission is a new National Commission to Investigate Youth Violence. It was created by unanimous vote of the U.S. Senate a couple of years back, so it's one of those special "high-powered" blue ribbon commissions, and as such may well include *two* guys who dated Madonna.

This commission was charged with determining what impact "violence in the media has on kids."

Will this have Hollywood shaking in its designer jeans? Will the arrayed might of TV, Radio and Print, and Internet head for the hills? Not likely. No matter how many commissions are appointed, there's not going to be a smoking-gun, finger-pointing, j'accuseatory single reason why kids are blowing one another away, nor a single Dr. Evil to scapegoat.

So while partially responsible parties continue to whine, "Who, me?" kids keep killing kids, blue ribbon commissions keep meeting and blue ribbon sales are through the roof.

Yes, Virginia, it's partially parents' fault. Some don't want to, are unqualified to or are unable to stand vigil for the daily assaults on the minds of their kids from violent entertainment, grotesque video games, shock radio, reality programming, reality itself and the most dangerous influence of all, peer pressure.

Yes, it's partially the entertainment industry's fault. Murder most foul, horror and atrocity can be artistic or exploitative. Creators of art rightfully enjoy the protection of the Bill of Rights. Purveyors of exploitative entertainment hide behind the protections of the Constitution instead of examining their consciences and doing what's right.

Yes, it's partially the media's fault. Newscasts, for instance, that have handed over journalistic responsibility to consultants who answer only to the bottom line are to blame for the daily carnage on newscasts.

Yes, it's partially the violent kids' fault. There are bad people in this world.

Yes, it's partially a society's fault that pays more than $100 million to seven-footers who can't hit free throws and subsistence wages to those charged with educating those genetically-challenged misfortunates whose growth plates closed early.

Yes, the intentional sleazing down, dumbing down and numbing down of that same society is partially to blame.

And yes, Tom Selleck and Charlton Heston, it's partially the fault of those members of the NRA who oppose sanity in the interest of clients' profit. But Tom, I think Rosie should have let you plug the movie first, before going Geraldo on you.

Maybe what's needed is a blue ribbon commission to assign percentages of blame. Or better yet, make blue ribbon commissions a thing of the Pabst. (Sorry.)

# Dreaded Cliché Shortfall Nipped in Bud

## Bad News and Other Bad News

# Dreaded Cliché Shortfall Nipped in the Bud
## (And You Know How Painful That Can Be)

Clichés have been the lifeblood of TV news ever since Hitler was in short pants. And they will continue to be such till the cows come home, or if the cows remain on tour, until pigs learn to fly. But even the best clichés eventually become passé. Finally, TV news is doing something about it

Under the little-known Banality Rotation Act of 2000, clichés are being temporarily removed from news circulation, and returned to common news usage years later. The system is based on the agricultural technique of crop rotation, only you don't have to eat your broccoli.

January 1, 2001. Phase One marked the temporary retirement of dozens of classic clichés including, "tired smoke-eaters," "the rain is good for the sassafras" and "residents reported hailstone-size golf balls."

Sen. Trent Lott, (R-Neptune), is an outspoken, though not by many, critic of the legislation.

"This law will result in a bigger bureaucracy, not to mention that stuffy, bloated feeling you get after too much pasta al dente. I yield the rest of my time to the distinguished gentleman from Beano, who coincidentally is named Al Dente. Al?"

But Senator Lott, whose blind pig recently unearthed a truffle, makes a good point. Could cliché removal risk dreaded cliché shortfall? Fortunately, that was headed off at the pass. Lawmakers anticipated that new, replacement clichés would be necessary for TV news to remain cutting edge.

A crack team of clichéd broadcasters and media historians soon formed a blue ribbon panel to devise new clichés and work them into circulation. And so in August 2001, in Phase Two, a second group of clichés was taken out of circulation and the first group of new clichés was inserted in their place.

The outgoing list included "a parent's worst nightmare," which was replaced by "worse than a parent's worst nightmare."

"Tragic death" was replaced by "fatal death." (Originally "calamitous death" was the panel's choice, but it was vetoed by Tom Brokaw, who couldn't pronounce the phrase without drooling.)

The popular tornado-victim MOS cliché "it sounded like a freight train" was retired in favor of "it sounded like a buncha stuff 'splodin' at once."

The old chestnut "ominous developments" was taken out of the mix for "apocalyptic developments." The cliché "old chestnut" was replaced in turn by "old party snack mix."

"Not in my backyard" proved one of the most challenging clichés to replace, according to the Cliché Committee. "Not in my hammock" was deemed too provincial. "Not in my shorts," "not in my wife's soufflé" and "not near my time-share" were tested and rejected before the panel picked "Not here, pal, or I'll sue your ass."

If you spot someone using any of the banned clichés on the air, you should report him to the FCC, if it's still in business.

A number of clichés have been updated to appeal to that youthful demographic advertisers so covet. A good example: "senseless shooting" has been changed to "a really def shooting."

Much work remains to be done. But the committee will be giving it 125 percent effort, which replaces 110 percent effort.

# Exclusive News!!!
# (Only in This Book!)

Are you sick and tired of hearing about "Exclusive!" news stories on the tube? Of course you are. (If you aren't, then just play along.)

"Exclusive!" is one of those consultant-driven hot buzz words, like "Live!" "Local!" or "Late-Breaking!" And by consultant-driven, I mean consultant-encouraged, not actually *driven*, as in "driven to drink." Although, to be honest, many a good newsman has been driven to drink by consultants.

"Exclusive!" has been abused, overused, overworked and whipped like a rented mule by TV news. (Now would be as good a time as any to remind our readers that no animals were injured in the production of this book.)

Understanding consultants the way I do—and trust me, I wish I didn't—I know TV news will continue to overwork the word "Exclusive!" But, come on, would I have written this piece if I didn't have suggestions to improve the situation? Of course not. So, you troublemakers in the back of the room, drop those rocks and bottles, get back to your seats and resume your knitting.

As exciting as the word "Exclusive!" is to news management and consultants (several of whom have had to leave the business due to uncontrollable priapism), there are more specific words that can sometimes be used in its stead. This can entice even more viewers by offering fresh yet familiar terms to describe upcoming stories.

We feel the new variants should be used whenever possible. (And by "we feel," of course, I mean "*me* feel." There isn't a squad of chimps hammering out these theories, you know, just me.)

**Inclusive!** A story that, for a change, actually includes facts.

**Reclusive!** An interview with a public figure who prefers to remain private, such as a one-on-one with J. D. Salinger.

**Unreclusive!** An interview with someone you can't get to shut up and go away, such as Kathie Lee Gifford or Madonna.

**B-clusive!** An exclusive story of so little interest it doesn't make the "A" block, and has fallen to the "B" block. Either that, or—and forgive me, for I have punned—your cameraman tripped over a wasp's nest and shot some footage before diving into a lake.

**Seeclusive!** We have some paparazzi video of a celebrity in a bikini.

**D-clusive!** We have some paparazzi video of Dolly Parton in a bikini.

**Feeclusive!** An exclusive we've paid for.

**Heclusive/Sheclusive!** Story about sexual discrimination, or an exclusive about someone famous who's changed sex.

**Meclusive!** A story only I care about.

**Kneeclusive!** An interview with a professional ballplayer who is not recovering from ACL surgery as quickly as expected and will miss the playoffs.

**Teeclusive!** Your sports guy, after several glasses of lunch, thinks he heard a locker attendant say that his cousin the caddie's sister's friend said she heard Tiger Woods may quit golf.

**E!clusive!** The E! Entertainment Network gang has finally nailed that long sought after "Where are they now?" interview with Jerry Mathers.

**Weeclusive!** (Scottish/Irish derivation) An exclusive that isn't such a big deal; i.e., "a wee little story that only we have."

**Zeeclusive!** The worst exclusive you can have; say, CNN's exclusive about the use of poison gas in Southeast Asia during the Vietnam War.

# Facts: No Longer Necessary for News?

Not too long ago, *NBC Nightly News* mentioned that a deceased woman had been found stuffed in the overhead bin of an airliner. It was part of a special story about how too much carry-on luggage was stretching the confines of overhead bins on airliners. And it really got your attention. At the end of the story, Tom Brokaw admitted the incident might never have happened; it might have been just an airborne urban legend. Still, a number of media people are upset about NBC's use of the story.

Some claim factually unproveable evidence was misused in the story, just to make a point and stir emotions. It's one thing to know "your luggage may have shifted during flight," quite another to find Granny slung across your Samsonite. These whiners and traditionalists say that the old-lady-stuffed-in-the-overhead-bin yarn should have been omitted entirely. *I* think the problem is that these old-timers have their head up their past, and for some reason aren't willing or able to make the factual adjustments needed to continue to make news the profitable juggernaut it is today.

Some would even claim anchor Tom Brokaw and the reporter might well have been canned over this in the old days. Well, duh. But by current news standards, inclusion of such an old wives' tale in a story comes under the acceptable heading of "close enough for network news." The admission that it was probably a whopper was unnecessary in my view. I mean, come on. Hundreds of thousands of flights every week. Surely, at some time somewhere someone put a dead ol' lady in with the overhead luggage. Just stands to reason.

It is my opinion that, in these modern times, entirely too much emphasis has been placed on accuracy in the news. I think it's time the public accepted the reality that news is no longer fact-driven. Facts impede flow, cause delays in getting to live shots, confuse the viewer, lead to unwanted litigation and are frequently hard to prove.

Instead of being so pessimistic, journalists should look on the bright side. With fewer facts involved, writing and video can be livelier and more viewer-friendly. With "digging" reduced, reporters will have time for more stories and will seldom have to work through lunch.

# Gray Lady Down

It was shortly before Christmas 1967. I was in the U.S. Air Force, stationed at Langley AFB, Virginia. My paternal grandmother, who lived near Washington, D.C., was driving down to Williamsburg for Christmas, her car filled with packages and pastries.

At a turn-off near Richmond, now circumvented by an Interstate, she turned left across traffic. She was hit by an oncoming car she did not see until it was too late.

My father called me with the news, said not to worry, she was in the hospital grumbling about the food. But within two days she was dead from internal bleeding. What followed was certainly the darkest Christmas our family had endured, particularly for my father.

His mother had raised him and his sister pretty much alone—his father left them when they were young—and she had a difficult life even after both children were fully grown. My father had recently found her an apartment in a pleasant little development a mile from where he lived. There she could putter in her garden, make cakes and pies for the neighbors and finally begin to enjoy life.

I remember she had a rep as a strong-willed Irish woman, given to fits of shouting and temper. Not easy to get along with, but that never held for me. As her only grandson, I always got a pass on whatever woes of the world were bothering her. She never once said a harsh word to me, nor I to her. She had a voice like a foghorn, and a no-nonsense attitude about life, but I thought of her as kind and loving and the maker of the best lemon meringue pies in the world.

How sad her death was, and how personal. Our grief for her was great and her loss deeply felt. It had devastated a family, brought unexpected pain. Private pain. No one outside the circle could feel it. Nor was there any need for them to do so. Each family has its own pain to deal with.

I hadn't thought about my grandmother or her death until recently, when a major media event here in Los Angeles reminded me of it. Someone else's grandmother had died making a left hand turn. She, too, was hit by traffic she did not see until it was too late. Her car, too, was filled with holiday packages, and her death took place shortly before the holiday season.

Unlike my grandmother, she died instantly. Unlike my grandmother, she died in the glare of a media spotlight. Over and over again. Her final instant of life shown for the entertainment of hundreds of thousands of strangers.

She was the lead on everybody's news that night not because of the life she lived but merely because of the way she died.

As car chases go, it was a doozy, the kind that makes grown station execs cry that it didn't happen during sweeps. A guy stole an SUV, then led cops and choppers on the customary high-speed pursuit. But instead of stopping and meekly surrendering, he slammed into the grandmother's car at about 90 mph.

The choppers had gotten it all, up close and personal. The victim was a 77-year-old woman who had been married 55 years. She was, we were informed, a "Holocaust survivor." She was headed, reporters speculated, for the post office to mail holiday packages. "Never had a chance," an eyewitness said. "Pushed her car a hundred feet down the road."

You don't have to tell the modern day newsie that this is emotional gold. It is first block, team coverage, 14-karat, Nielsen-lovin', bright and shiny, lead-story gold.

And L.A. TV didn't drop the ball. On the early news, Channel Two, the Station of the People, first braced the audience by warning that the upcoming video was "graphic and tragic." Such warnings, as you may know, are designed to scare off the squeamish, deflect media criticism, and, most importantly, tip off viewers to cease fixing dinner, reading the mail, or playing with the kids and pay attention. It's the equivalent of soaps and game shows hitting you with music, bells and whistles to warn the inattentive to look up *now!*

True to their promise, *ka-pow!!!* There it was, in full, shocking, graphic detail.

The footage was indeed graphic and tragic, but alas, over in an instant. What to do? Real-time exploitation won't hack it in the big city, so the tape was rerun again in tragic and graphic super slo-mo. *Kaaaaaaaaaaaaaa-pooooooooooowwwwwwwwwwww!!!!!!!!!!!*

Every news station ran the crash. Everyone went "live from the scene of the tragedy," never mind that it had happened hours ago.

Some ran footage of paramedics getting ready to move the body. You could see the victim's gray hair as she lay on the concrete by her car.

Channel Five and others used the crash in their pre-show tease.

Channel Eleven warned us its video was "graphic."

Channel Thirteen described the video as "shocking."

Channels Four and Seven led with it, too.

I caught only one newscast Friday night where a station—my former Alma Mater KCAL-9—did *not* lead with the crash. Were they distracted by President-elect Bush's activities? The power crisis in California? The plight of the poor at Christmas? An attack of conscience?

Naaaah.

KCAL's lead story on their Eight O'Clock News was the critical information that the University of Southern California had hired a new football coach that day. The car chase was next.

Did anyone, did one single news director or show producer pipe up and say, we have the video, but out of respect for the dead woman and her family, we will not use it?

Not successfully, and I think I know why. These people have rent or mortgages to pay and mouths to feed. Anyone who might raise issues of taste, civility, humanity or exploitation has long since been silenced or run out of town.

Besides, it's not personal, it's just the New News. This was no real, flesh-and-blood person to L.A. TV. She wasn't famous before she died, and no one will remember her until it's time to trot out the old video for some new car chase tragedy, when anchor faces turn somber again.

The woman was just tonight's TV news footage. It was merely entertainment for the ghoulish, the mawkish, the thrill-seekers and knuckle draggers TV news has created as its demographically desirable audience. Baby wants sugar? Give baby sugar.

Was the footage mesmerizing? Sure. It was a hot-button action-package, with a genuine ka-pow money shot for the New TV News. It was a no-brainer for those who know ratings are what matters, and that to get ratings, you gotta stir the emotions. Give 'em blood, sweat, tears and fears.

Car chases are the coin of the realm here in L.A., and rapidly gaining footholds elsewhere. Most end without incident. The grandmother crash had the double advantage of entertainment now, and serving as a hook to get viewers to stay tuned during car-chases to come. It was the payback for all the suspects who surrendered meekly, for all the times the chase ended and nobody died. TV critics may crank out a view-with-alarm column. But in essence, it's really just business as unusual, the norm for news in L.A., and coming soon to a station near you, if it hasn't already.

But I think about what I would have felt like if my grandmother's death had been put on public display for entertainment purposes. I think how much more pain it would have caused my father.

And I realize just how far news has descended, and suddenly my mind is repeating a lyric from an old limbo record.

"How low can you go?" the man asks. "How low can you go?"

# TV: A Big Tease Followed by an Anticlimax

News teases are way out of hand. Many of them don't make sense. Some out-and-out lie. Too many have a terminal case of the cutes, where the seriousness of the story gives way to the tease-writer's opportunity to turn what he or she thinks is a clever phrase.

I once heard a news tease about a teen who had touched an electrical wire and was in critical condition. The tease went: "Coming up next, a local teen gets the shock of his life." Since the tease appeared on the station at which I then worked—and I was in the newsroom at the time—I decided to visit the tease writer.

I asked her why she wrote a cheesy, trivializing pun to describe the life-threatening accident that happened to the young man, and what she thought the boy's parents might think of her tease.

She agreed it was inappropriate, apologized, left the business and joined a convent. (Okay, the first two, anyway.)

I heard an even more absurd tease shortly after the presidential "election" of 2000. One evening, a KABC-TV anchor was doing a radio spot to tease that evening's TV newscast. It would run on a local newsradio station.

It was a big news day, including then candidate Dick Cheney's going into the hospital for a ticker tune-up. The news tease took place in the late afternoon, some eight hours after Cheney's chest pains were first reported.

The spot ran right after a detailed update on Cheney's condition. As breaking news goes, the chest pains story had whiskers and a Medicare card. You pretty much had to have been under a rock all day to miss news of Cheney's heart attack.

There were plenty of opportunities to stop or rewrite the tease. Likely it was written by a newswriter, approved by at least one supervisor, and certainly read and understood by the anchor who did the tease.

"Also coming up at five o'clock, we'll tell you which vice presidential candidate had a minor heart attack today."

(Isolated incident? Later that night, on Fox, I heard the "we'll tell you which veep candidate had the heart attack later" tease again. Of course, that's Fox.)

What did KABC expect? Rufus to turn to Gomer and ask, "Gosh, I wunner which one it wuz? I guess I better turn in that Channel Seven tonight and watch."

Started me to wondering what teases we might have heard had television been invented earlier—much earlier.

> Did you hear it? We'll tell you what that Big Bang was all about and what it might mean to the universe. Exclusive coverage from Earth!

> Later, our senior science reporter, Og the Caveman, tries to explain why we're seeing so few dinosaurs around these days.

> Coming up, He called Himself a Savior, but He had a tough lesson *hammered* home today. We're there, live from Calvary.

> Good news and bad news for Christopher Columbus. He's found land, but it sure isn't India.

> And coming up, we'll tell you what certain red-coated army bit the big one and may be setting sail soon for England.

Well, now we may know why a certain Frenchman who came up *short* in Russia has been keeping his hand in his tunic. Hint: Moscow in winter is no day at the beach.

Coming up! More live coverage of the assassination tonight at Ford's Theater. Plus our entertainment guru has a review of "Our American Cousin."

What major nation had its battleships sunk in a surprise raid today? Stay tuned, it's a *pearl* of a story.

Did you hear it? We'll tell you what that Big Bang was all about and what it might mean to the universe. Exclusive coverage from Hiroshima.

# A Midair Collision Can
# Spoil Your Whole Day

Los Angeles is a city where anyone with a set of car keys and a "Darwin Was Wrong" tattoo can hijack a television newscast for hours at a time. Just one no-stop bonehead doing ninety on the freeway is soon pursued by a dozen black and whites, and almost as many news choppers overhead.

When hot on a car chase, this airborne swarm appears to be a demolition derby waiting to happen. But the aviation skills of the L.A. pilots make Van Richthofen's Flying Circus look like Monty Python's.

The men at the controls must follow the chase, report the story, avoid colliding with other airborne Cuisinarts and explain fuel flow to an assignment desk intern who suggests he "save gas" by "turning off that big overhead fan."

The pilot must also communicate with police, air traffic control, other choppers and an on-air anchor who asks if he can see if the suspect is smoking filtered or unfiltered cigarettes.

All that, and looking pretty and smiling into the camera for tosses and tags, monitoring the onboard monitor, applying Cover Girl's creamy bronze "Air Stud" makeup, and twirling his handlebar to proper specs.

Most of these pilots are amazingly good, even while dodging rioters' bullets, or in the worst weather conditions. They've been known to alert the world that a truck driver is being beaten by a mob, show the progression of wildfires to those in their path and pluck out the occasional flash flood victim.

In addition, they must suppress their gag reflex when ordered to give you're-airborne-anyway-so-we-might-as-well-go-live coverage of garage fires, fender-benders and the retrieval of a sack that "might" contain a dead infant.

I'm not implying that all TV helicopter pilots are as battle-tested as the Los Angeles breed. I wouldn't be shocked to learn that some stations hire the first guy who knows that the collective isn't a church offering basket.

But pilots, helicopter and fixed-wing, don't get enough props (no pun intended). They are among the first to contribute to the common good, be they firefighters, hurricane hunters, air rescue, CAP guys looking for missing hikers or media pilots.

All that being said, the very nature of car chases, and the multi-tasking put on the chopper jocks makes a mid-air collision inevitable, just a matter of time. It is unsafe for the residents below—and unconscionable—especially considering the nature of the non-news that is being covered.

# What the Anchor Will Never *Ever* Say

I've been listening to local anchors for years now. Most of their words are scripted. But sometimes ad libs, often used as transition devices, baffle me. For instance, after a field reporter has thrown it back from a live shot about police finding the dismembered remains of a convent of cloistered nuns, why does the anchor inevitably say: "Thank you for that, Bob"? What in God's name is he thankful for? And what if the guy's name isn't Bob?

Mostly, with the fast-paced news formats consultants have required, anchors just spit out short phrases as they race along to the next drive-by victim. "You bet," "Stay on it," "Nice job," are about as profound as these get.

As a counterpoint to that, I sat down the other day and came up with a list of comments I've never heard anchors say but would like to:

> Welcome to the six o'clock news, I'm Biff Schnauzer along with Raisonette Johnson. We can't stand each other.

> It's probably just some idiot looking to be famous, so we're gonna cut away from that car chase for the latest on school bond issues.

Thanks for the live shot. But next time, Larry, instead of *asking* a bunch of barely coherent onlookers what *they* think about the building collapse, why don't you do some reporting and ask someone who may actually know something about why it happened?

I suppose that was a pretty good story about a pot-bellied sow nursing a litter of kittens. But what the hell has that got to do with news?

Sorry we didn't ask the victim's grieving mother what it's like to find her young son ruthlessly murdered in the family driveway, but we didn't want to invade her privacy.

Sorry for that mistake, but you see, I usually wander in around three, so I never really get a chance to check this crap before I read it.

We'll be back with more alleged news right after this.*

Sorry for the dull news tonight folks, but sweeps are coming and we're saving our best titillation for then.

Wow, that story on teachers' pay raises was only a minute and five seconds long. I didn't get anything out of it, did you?

You know where we got that story? We sent an intern down to the newsstand to pick up the latest tabloids.

Walter, great live shot, but I've forgotten the question you gave me to ask you so you look brighter than you actually are.

---

*This is a ringer. Someone actually said this on air, and was reportedly fired for his trouble.

Wait, Bob, if we're supposed to be live, local and late-breaking, why are you giving us a taped piece about yesterday's news in a city five hundred miles away?

Hey, you're not the only one who was confused by that last story. But you see, to save money we let our veteran reporters go and replaced them with people who couldn't find their ass with both hands.

# Like, Now, It's Now
# Time to Go Live, Now

*This is a response to a letter to* ShopTalk *by "Tom," asking why reporters use the word "now" so often in live shots. I did some anecdotal research and came up with the answer.*

I've been reading the letters here for weeks without inspiration. Same old drivel, same tired old drudgery.

Nothing but missives about issues in the Elian Gonzalez case. And letters arguing the importance of journalistic integrity. (Hey, get a life, okay?) Writers pondering whether television should show dead bodies during the First Anniversary Columbine Media Circus & Ratings-Driven Hypefest. Correspondents asking "How many ethics does it take to screw up a newscast?" (None. That's the consultant's job.)

Now, Tom, you ask a question that lights my fire. A question I feel qualified, even compelled, to answer.

You want to know why reporters speak differently live than when packaged? Specifically, you write: "Ever notice how many reporters begin their close [after the internal package] in a live shot by saying, 'Now . . .'? You don't normally hear that on the close standup on a produced package when the copy has been written or recorded. . . . Why on a live shot?"

Okay, Tom, here's the explanation, based on real factual statistical data I just made up.

**37 percent** of TV reporters say "now" when coming back live from a package because they've lost contact with the control room and don't know when to start talking. They can't tell if their shooter's hand signals are cueing them, beating off a gnat attack, or practicing sign language. In some cases the reporter is asking "Do I talk now?" and his audio man, –ister Upcut, has opened his mike late.

**23 percent** of TV reporters say "now" because they're "live," and it actually is "now" not "then," whereas the event they're covering now took place back then. Perhaps six hours have passed since the drive-by, but the desk sent him because the Boys in Research say the audience will tune out if exposed to meaningful news.

**14 percent** because the reporter is drunk.

**10 percent** for religious reasons.

**9 percent** as an homage to the National Organization for Women.

The remaining seven percent includes miscellaneous, "no opinion" and misinterpretation of natural phenomena.

As always, your mileage may vary, and my percentages are off because (1) I can't add, and (2) I don't really give a damn. I mean, come on, you know this particular essay is just made up stuff, right? Oh, there's lots of juicy real information elsewhere in the book, but this one is primarily filler, kind of a valley so you can better see the peaks. Don't get on my case, everyone does that. Even Dave Barry, and Benchley, and don't even get me started on Andy Rooney. And look at Robin Williams. The guy's been in some great flicks, but a lot of them are stinko, with a capital Stink. So go pick on someone your own size, before I call the militia.

# All Along, "Pravda" Really Meant "Naked"

I love it when a confluence of events presents a problem and then solves it almost immediately. I mean, I can't do all the heavy lifting around here.

This problem began during the heart of the Cold War. The very first satellite, called *Sputnik*, was launched by the Soviet Union and shook America awake to the huge missile gap that had opened between the United States and the U.S.S.R. In a media development that put the "I" in Irony, the same kind of shocking event recently established the former Soviet Union's supremacy over the U.S. in an area we had dominated for years—TV news.

It was an unexpected leap forward by a once-fettered society, and if you've ever had your society fettered, you wouldn't be sitting there with that smug grin. Or perhaps you would. I don't know you that well, and after seeing that mess that you call an office, I'm not sure I want to. Anyway, breakup of the Soviet Union or no, we were convinced no former Communist country could touch us, especially in news. Typical American arrogance bit us in the ass once again, and if you don't think that can hurt, well, you just don't know American asses.

America had long ruled the airwaves, coming up with innovation after innovation. Live shots, news teases, satellite trucks, consultants, résumé reels, StormWatchCast weather, wacky outtakes in sports, walk and talks, move and grooves, sweeps series, digital graphics, chrome and aluminum sets, capped anchor teeth and anchorboobs, clothing allowances, Anchor-Strength Hairspray, smiling, attractive anchorhumans everywhere you looked—it was all U.S.A.

Meanwhile Soviet, and later, post-U.S.S.R., television broadcasts lagged badly. Whenever there was big news out of the Kremlin, you'd see some scowling anchorette, looking like a Euro version of Miss Hannigan from *Annie*, anchoring their news. Grim faced, built like linebackers, Russian anchorettes scared the free world and Bolsheviks in the street. But all that changed in a sudden, brilliant Russian stroke, almost overnight.

Russian researchers realized the prohibitive costs of competing with American newscasts in hardware technology. Instead, with one startling breakthrough, the Russians have, for the first time ever, seriously threatened American leadership in news.

How did they do it? They started doing the news with nude anchors. Better yet, anchors who started out fully clothed, then who, in a creative reinterpretation of the term "news tease," began stripping during the newscast. And unlike the steel wool panty–clad nightmare anchorettes of yore, these new stripping anchorettes were babes. *Playboyski*-level females. Ratings jumped.

America was caught completely off guard by this electronic Pearl Harbor. Reaction in the United States was immediate. Editorialists, columnists and men on the street at first looked askance, then began to view with alarm, before demanding a quick-fix solution.

Then-President Bill Clinton promised to personally look into the situation. Soon, echoing the "we will put a man on the moon by 1970" call to action of President Kennedy, he suggested an all-out bipartisan attempt to match or surpass Russian topless news by 2010. After his inauguration, President George W. Bush quickly promised to take the proposal "under adviserary" and report back after his nap.

Yet the very networks that would most benefit from such a return to glory remained strangely silent. There were naysayers, also, those who believed the country would be better off investing its money and energies elsewhere—better technology, more satellite trucks for better and more far-ranging live shots.

"Why focus on stripping anchors?" one broadcaster who requested anonymity asked. "They're just breasts. You can do better than that on the Internet."

But others argued TV was losing viewership to the Internet every day, and if it ever hoped to compete with the new technologies, it would have to strike boldly and decisively.

Still months went by with little being done. Blouses stayed in place; jackets remained buttoned. Not a flash of lingerie was seen. In fact, a TV journalism web site reported that there might be a counter-reaction here in the U.S.

"On air sometimes I look too busty—I don't like it," one obviously distressed anchorette wrote to the web site *Medialine*. "Is there a particular brand of bra that really supports and flattens you down, making things less obvious??? Who has had some positive results at minimization???"

There were a number of responses designed to help the woman hide her assets.

"Hold your scripts up higher when you're on camera. It hides your chest and it's a lot cheaper than a boob job," one journalist responded.

"Any sports bra also should be able to help," another suggested.

"Get a minimizer bra. Then, take a good hard look at the suits and blazers in your closet. Toss out the double-breasted styles (no pun intended). Then get rid of anything tight. Tight makes you look busty. Go for classic styles with minimal detailing. And use distraction. Pull attention away from your bust by wearing simple scarves or pins."

Another amply endowed anchor suggested a little preparation could go a long way.

"I . . . had the worst seat at the anchor desk for monitor shots . . . a side shot which accentuated my chest size! Before the news, I would check the monitor to see where I could place my arm on the desk to hide my boobs. A desperate move, but it worked."

Worked? At what? Keeping America a second-rate news nation? People are turning away from the news in droves. And the Russian advances seem more obvious as America lags.

I wouldn't suggest it's some kind of unpatriotic skullduggery or part of a Communist plot, but news consultants have done a lot to help the Rooskies. With their emphasis on focus groups and research, News consultants have helped drive people away from local news by encouraging gimmickry, shallowness, live shot mania, high story count. The result: consistent, mind-blowing day-to-day dullness. Come on, you bozos. Do a real focus group. Ask men if they like tits. Ask women if they like buff nude guys. How complicated is that?

Even Canada is ahead of us. Oh, the *horror*! Our-north-of-the-border neighbors have a half-hour stripcast, where anchors—they're called "presenters" there—strip while reporting the news. Not on TV—yet—but on a web site. According to *Variety*, it has grown at an amazing 53 percent a week and in February of 2001 had 5.5 million hits a month.

Our progress? In January 2001, WB station WPIX in New York, used its morning "newscast" in a manner that appears to be a step forward. The anchor, one Lynn White, has taken to displaying her bellybutton on the air. Also, weatherchick Linda Church was observed shaking her booty to the strains of "Gettin' Jiggy Wit' It."

A breakthrough? Hardly. We as a nation have a long way to go. But it's a start. But I believe topless news is within reach. I believe that this nation should commit itself to achieving the goal, before this decade is out, of landing topless women in the set, and returning them safely to their offices.

# The Unnecessary
# Agony of Adrienne

During one of their early evening newscasts, KABC *Eyewitness News* in L.A. did a live shot from a golf course. As near as I could surmise, the story was about the fact it was a cloudy day in Los Angeles. Usually, it is sunny at this time of year in Los Angeles, not cloudy—except at night, when it's mostly dark.

The report included an MOS from a golfer who explained he preferred playing golf when it was 80 degrees and sunny but would play even when it was cloudy and cooler, which it was today. Later in the newscast, KABC's effervescent nice guy weatherman, Dallas Raines, confirmed that indeed it was a cloudy day, but that there would be "plenty of sunshine for the weekend."

The same newscast also included a kicker about a flock of mimes (Gaggle of mimes? Silence of mimes?) who rode a scary new roller coaster without making a peep. The anchors then happychatted about how they could hear the rollercoaster and background noise on the tape, but indeed, the mimes were silent. Good show, mimes, the anchors said enthusiastically. I think the rollercoaster was located somewhere other than L.A., because the skies behind the silent mimes were blue, not cloudy.

And then there was the "coverage" of the accident that critically injured KABC reporter Adrienne Alpert on Monday, May 22, 2000. Miss Alpert was severely injured when the microwave mast of the truck she was in came in close contact with high-power lines. She was critically burned, and among other things, had to have her foot and several fingers amputated. Her long and painful recovery continues as this is being written some nine months after the accident. She went back on air in 2001.

The coverage consisted of a brief update of her condition and a VO/SOT of the KABC news team giving blood to the Red Cross, which had come to the station to get it. News people are very, very busy people.

After the video of the KABC employees giving blood, one anchor allowed as how it was his first time giving blood. Another noted that "it sure makes you get over your fear of needles when you're doing good for a co-worker."

What there was not on KABC, unless I missed it, or on any other station, unless I missed it, was reporting about the accident investigation itself. I have a few questions that remain unanswered.

Why did the accident happen? How can such an accident be prevented in the future? Is there a caution placard by the mast controls? Has the station considered and rejected available devices to warn of potential danger? Is there a remote device to enable the operator to step outside and eyeball the mast as it's being raised?

Did someone in management contribute to the danger by applying pressure to make the live shot? Did the fact that the accident occurred near the end of a hard-fought sweeps period contribute to a need to be first with the story? Was the van delayed coming from another story? Had the reporter or shooter ever missed a live shot before for safety reasons? Was the reporter's contract up soon? Might she have been reluctant to press safety issues for fear of non-renewal?

What did the driver do after she was apparently warned by the victim before the accident that they might be in danger? Did she leave the truck and check for clearance? Was she aware that electrical wires need not be physically touched by the mast to cause deadly injury? Is there even a formal investigation going on? If so, who is conducting it?

Was there a written checklist to be followed? After all, every time an airliner lands, one pilot asks and receives confirmation from the other that the landing gear is down and locked. Just because most live shots, like most landings, are uneventful doesn't mean they are not dangerous if proper procedures aren't in place and followed. The very instincts that drive a reporter and cameraperson to get a story are often in conflict with common sense.

During my own on-air experience, some live shots seemed unnecessarily risky through no fault of the crew. An example: Minimum crew requirement for a live shot was two. Sometimes that meant the second person would be messengered over at the last second. Meanwhile one person, not two, had to run cable, set up lights, put up the mast, get the signal, replace a faulty audio line, communicate with the desk and the receive site, replace a dead brick, check talent's makeup and hair, feed back B-roll for the tease, edit the package, retrieve talent to call a PA with the chyron list, and try not to get hit by passing traffic.

So I guess the biggest question is, why is news of this tragic accident being reduced to blood drives and hospital reports? If it had been a plane crash, there already would have been hard questions asked and theories expounded. News coverage can change policies and improve conditions by the simple act of exposure itself.

# Let's Honor News Directors for What They Do

Sometimes solutions to complex problems are as simple as the nose on your face, if not nearly so cute. At least, most solutions seem simple to me, but then I've lived in the land of La-La for ten consecutive years now. Because Southern California living reduces the IQ by ten points a year, my once-lofty 182 IQ is down to an even 125.

Where was I? Right. Some of you might have read about the TV station promotions guy who got caught rigging a giveaway so his mother-in-law would win a $27,000 truck and then give it to him. (Insert your own mother-in-law joke here.)

So the bozo is fined $10,000, and sentenced to 60 days in the pokey and his 15 minutes of fame.

But here's the topper. Hizzoner also ordered the guy to show up at a Rice University football game wearing a sign that reads: "I am a liar, a coward and a thief. I rigged the Channel 51 contest so my mother-in-law would win the pickup truck and give it to me." Assuming some higher court doesn't overrule on the grounds that sentencing someone to a Rice University football game is cruel and unusual punishment, I think it's time for TV news to get in on the ground floor of a trend that could change the course of television history.

The public, politicians, sages, soothsayers, do-gooders and grandstanders have been urging TV news to clean up its act for years. They fear, as do many of us, that violence and sexual content in lieu of actual journalism lead to a dangerous increase in violence, promiscuity and blue ribbon commissions assigned to study the issue.

I say the inflictors of sleaze and violence on the tube should be forced to own up to it publicly. (This kind of punishment started with the legendary novel nobody read called *The Scarlet Letter*, by Willem Dafoe, which held fornicating foremothers up to ridicule and didn't do a lot for Demi Moore's acting career.)

I say, make news directors go out in public wearing sandwich boards that read: "I'm So-and-So, proud conveyor of a five-part series on hookers with inverted nipples."

Or, "I'm Hoosywhatsis, and my willingness to pander is the reason we lead our market in live, local and ludicrous first-block drive-bys."

Logically, when they do right, they should be encouraged to take the credit. In that case, they could wear signs reading: "I'm the guy whose first block was about educational issues. Ask me about my forwarding address."

Dang, I don't even have room to mention that mom-in-law ratted out the truck guy and got off scot-free.

# The Trouble with TV News,
# Wrapped in a Blue Ribbon

*In the late nineties, the Radio and Television News Directors Foundation (RTNDF) did a survey that came up with some surprising statistics. I don't believe in statistics unless they're used to prove a point I agree with. Here follows an exchange between RTNDA president Barbara Cochran and me on the pages of* ShopTalk. *I started it, so me first.*

> Two out of three Americans rank their local TV news as "good" or "excellent," according to a new study commissioned by the Radio and Television News Directors Foundation.
>
> —RTNDF News Release

If the RTNDA and its Foundation really take solace in the fact their self-sponsored survey indicates that two out of three respondents rate TV news coverage "good" or "excellent," they ignore some troublesome facts.

For one, it appears the survey disregards those who've abandoned watching TV news completely, a not inconsiderable sum who might have a different opinion from those surveyed. For another, should anyone really be that surprised that increasingly sensationalistic, tabloidy and crime-ridden broadcasts satisfy viewers in an age when professional wrestling and Jerry Springer are achieving their greatest ratings *ever*? I'd bet two out of three babies would prefer candy to baby formula, too.

When you visit RTNDF's web site and look into it further, you'll find the bright face RTNDF paints is not so bright after all.

Of those surveyed, only 14 percent of those who watch local news consider it "excellent"(highest rating). And only one in five viewers who watch local news considered news coverage "very fair" (highest rating).

If those figures are satisfactory to the RTNDA, I suggest the RTNDA may be part of the problem, not the solution to attaining high local news broadcast standards.

*The response came from RTNDA president Barbara Cochran, speaking in the imperial "we," presumably for the RTNDA.*

We're sorry that Mr. Corcoran misconstrued our intentions, but grateful for him pointing out to *ShopTalk* readers that our survey raises some important questions.

To recap, RTNDF recently commissioned a survey that said, among other things, that Americans rely heavily upon local television for their news and give local news programs higher quality ratings than other forms of news. The study also said that Americans are becoming increasingly skeptical about the accuracy of anything they hear or see on the news and they question the motives behind some of the stories that run.

The digested form of the news release that ran in *ShopTalk* naturally did not reflect the whole picture. Our study went into many areas—such as hidden camera use and the perceived political leanings of reporters—some of them indicating trouble spots for the news media in general and local TV news in particular. That is why we are using the survey results as a springboard to a three-year exploration of credibility and news ethics.

The project—which is designed to measure the level of public trust instead of relying on subjective guesses—will include a survey about radio news; 18 forums of news directors, journalists and the public; training sessions for journalists on decision-making and news judgment; and another comprehensive survey in two years to assess any progress. We undertook this project because we acknowledged there was a need to get the public's input and to explore the way we are perceived.

The three-year project RTNDF has undertaken is designed to engage the entire local news community in a discussion of what needs to be done to earn and keep the public's trust. The survey was a starting point and we will continue to provide updates as the project progresses. To see the complete survey results, including the summary and the raw data, see [*www.rtnda.org/issues/survey.pdf*].

*I then responded to Ms. Cochran:*

So, RTNDA's most recent survey into what the heck's wrong with TV news has resulted in RTNDA sponsoring a brand spanking new study into what the heck's wrong with TV news, with yet another survey to be taken after the first two years of the new three-year study.

This takes us several years past the millennium, and—if I remember my scientific method—will inevitably spin off additional studies and surveys to try to determine once and for all just what the heck is wrong with TV news.

Might one respectfully suggest RTNDA is studying the root structure of trees when the forest is on fire?

Let me help. To save time, here's some unscientific anecdotal evidence of what the heck may be wrong with TV news.

- At the station in a top five market, a newscast led with a story about someone using a video camera to peek up the skirts of women in local department store dressing rooms. Because the original footage was unavailable, the station utilized crotch-cam to re-enact the crime.
- In 1996, the very night before the national elections for the presidency, every station in Los Angeles led its local news with the story that entertainer Michael Jackson either got a woman pregnant, or married or divorced her, or she had the baby. (Can't remember which; there's been unending coverage of Michael and his sex life.)
- In the number two market, I recently saw a wet-behind-the-ears reporter do her live standup while simultaneously putting a few

stray hairs back in place. One problem: she used the hand with her microphone in it. Fortunately she didn't brain herself with her pie-plate–sized mic logo, but it made her report into an audio roller coaster.

- Whereas "if it bleeds, it leads" was once an aberration, it is increasingly the norm. Night after night, some poor bastard is standing LIVE!! near the latest drive-by, car crash or home invasion, filling ninety seconds of first block with "police are puzzled," "neighbors shocked" and "the story is developing." Then in lieu of actual reporting, viewers get interviews with police officials, hospital spokespersons and the ubiquitous MOS. The MOS will say "he was a quiet boy," "I can't believe it, I mean, like, you know, it's unbelievable," or for that matter, "I'm a little teapot, short and stout" if the MOS thought it would get him on the tube.

- Sweeps series continue to do their thrice-annual sleaze wallow, presenting the latest twist on the twisted that the boys in marketing or station consultants think will play to the largest audience. The lives of strippers, druggies, breast-implanted women whose surgery went wrong, horribly wrong, philandering spouses and teenage mutant ninja hookers—about whom local news couldn't care less a month ago—are suddenly the focus of attention, complete with razzmatazz video, music and oh-so-tantalizing near-nudity.

- And let us not forget the in-depth coverage of sitcoms which coincidentally run that very night on that very channel on that very network.

I could provide many more non-scientific, flawed but close-enough-for-local-news examples. And do it in less than three days, let alone three years.

Oh, did I mention live car chases?

# Index

---